The Eyes of a Chef

KITCHEN TALES ON FOOD & FAITH

Fred L. Raynaud, C.E.C., C.C.A.

CELI Publication
A Cook for Christ

Copyright © 2014 by Fred L. Raynaud.

All rights reserved. This book is protected by the copyright laws of the United States of America. This book may not be copied or reprinted for commercial gain or profit. The use of short quotations or occasional page copying for personal or group study is permitted and encouraged. Permission will be granted upon request. Unless otherwise identified, Scripture quotations taken from the New King James Version. Scripture taken from the New King James Version®. Copyright © 1982 by Thomas Nelson, Inc. Used by permission. All rights reserved. Emphasis within Scripture quotations are the author's own. Please note that the author capitalizes certain pronouns in Scripture that refer to the Father, Son, and Holy Spirit, and may differ from some authors and publishers' styles. Take note that the name satan and related names are not capitalized. The author chooses not to acknowledge him, even to the point of violating grammatical rules.

Fred Raynaud/The Eyes of a Chef
www.EyesofaChef.com

Ordering Information:
Quantity sales. Special discounts are available on quantity purchases by corporations, associations, and others. For details, contact the "Special Sales Department" at the address above.

The eyes of a Chef/Fred Raynaud. —1st ed.
ISBN 978-0-9892811-6-4

Contents

Forward 7
   This Book 7

Preface 9
   God is in the Kitchen 9

Introduction 19

The Parable of the Sower 25

A Community of Believers 37

Salvation 51
   What is an Emulsifier? 54
   The Process 58

Hunger for God 63

Spiritual Growth 73
   I Knead You! 79

The Bread of Life 83
   The story of the first Passover 86

O' Bethlehem 89

Sanctification 105

Dreams & Visions 117

Poverty 125

What Can We Do As Christians?	132
Servants	137
Last Word	149
About the Author	159

To my best friend...
Jan Raynaud

"The most excellent method of going to God is that of doing our common business without any view of pleasing people but purely for the love of God."

- Brother Lawrence

Forward

"Food for the body is not enough. There must be food for the soul."

- Dorothy Day

This Book

"And let us not grow weary while doing good, for in due season we shall reap if we do not lose heart."

- Galatians 6:9

This book is a special book for me. You could say it is a rewrite, as it is born out of my earlier release: "Reflections from the Kitchen" (out of print). However, it is more than a rewrite, it is a recommitment, a letter to my King regarding my dedication to Christ and His eternal mercy and grace. "Reflections" was written the year following my son Jamisen's passing away. It was written in the comingling of my grief, faith, and profession. Jamisen worked for me in the kitchen at the Resort & Club at Little Harbor and for most of his life he was beside me in my culinary journey. In an unexpected way, Reflections helped me through a very difficult time. Yet, in reflecting back, I believe it was written "out of season" and before its time.

"Eyes of a Chef" is not a cookbook. You won't find any recipes between its pages. What you will find is a look at Christ and the dynamic themes of Christianity through the lens of cookery and the kitchen. The book is more of a devotional than topical in nature. The book takes you on a parabolic journey where culinary tales and life experiences reflect the dynamic truth of Scripture. It is a journey into the realm of the culinary arts with our eyes turned upward, towards Christ and His kingdom. It is a look at Christ as well as creation. It is a buffet table full of little morsels, chapters to cause you to ponder upon the richness of all that Christ is, as seen through the eyes of a Chef.

Each chapter is named after a Biblical concept or theme with the subtitle pointing to the culinary lens that illustrates that truth. Dive in and enjoy. I pray that the Lord will bless you as you sift through the issues of life.

    Fred Raynaud, C.E.C., C.C.A.

Preface

"Let us study the visible creation as we will; take the anatomy of the smallest animal; look at the smallest grain of corn that is planted in the earth, and the manner in which its germ produces and multiplies; observe attentively the rosebud, how carefully it opens to the sun and closes at its setting; and we shall see more skill and design than in all the works of man."

- François Fénelon (1651-1715)

God is in the Kitchen

Inspiration is all around you. It can come from many places and take many forms. I am a history buff and history has inspired more than I can tell. I love to study historical events and people from the past. I like to imagine walking in someone else's shoes and imagine the people, the times, culture, and the lives of those who came before me. I must tell you about a man who profoundly changed the way I work in the kitchen and look at the culinary arts.

He was a cook by trade, or at least a cook for a good portion of his life. His name was Nicholas Herman (1605?-1691). Later he was given the name Brother Lawrence of the Resurrection, due to his lay-ministry at a monastery in Paris. No, he was not a culinary giant. He did not usher in some newfound way to food preparation. Nor, was he on the cutting edge of a culinary revolution. He was not a forerunner to cuisine, as we know it. Yet, a giant he was, for it was said of him by Mother Saint Thérèse of Avila that, *"the Lord walks among the pots and pans."*

He was a humble man who lived three hundred years before I was born. He did not make a major impact on the world of his day, though behind the scenes, from the poor to society's elite, he touched many. In fact, Abbé de Beaufort published his writings, consisting of conversations and letters, just after his death. They were printed in two volumes: Maximes Spirituelles (1692) and Moeurs et Entretiens du Frère Laurent (1694). Later they were re-edited into a small book entitled *"The Practice of the Presence of God."* It is here, in this little book that I, like millions before me, were moved by this cook's simple passion for God and a call to intimacy with Christ. In his writings, we discover his secret to *"the practice of the presence of God."* His method was simple, unceasingly he prayed and meditated on the Lord. He sought out and saw the splendor of His glorious presence in everything he did.

When I first read the words of Brother Lawrence, something inside me stirred. I wanted to know more about him, who he was, what he did. I wanted to know what lead him to the heartbeat of Christ. In reality, I wanted what he had. In my heart, I have always desired a walk with Christ that was closer than faith alone. I have never been content with warming a pew. Saying, "Yes I believe, and that is enough," never was enough. I wanted more of Him. As Moses, I desired to see His face... to see His Glory. I wanted to walk with Jesus as one would walk with a best friend, a wife, or a father.

This desire arose from deep inside me. I was stirred to seek the Lord with all that is within me... as if the deep places of my heart were crying out to the deep places of His. I desired to know God in the deepest sense of the word. I wanted to walk with Him in a profound way, beyond faith, beyond church, beyond religion. I wanted what I saw expressed in the writings of this humble seventeenth century cook.

This was not a new desire I was feeling. This was my heart's ambition the moment I came to Christ. I had found the lover of my soul and I would never let him go. My desire the moment Jesus saved me from the depth of my despair was to follow Him. The difference however, was *how* Brother Lawrence expressed it. He had put into words, and into action, what I had been feeling for a long time. Brother Lawrence had discovered the secret of being one with Christ.

In the gospel of John, before Jesus went to the cross, he prayed to the Father a marvelous prayer and in that prayer spoke of an incredible oneness with Him and His children.

> *"...I in them, and You in Me; that they may be made perfect in one, and that the world may know that You have sent Me, and have loved them as You have loved Me"*
>
> - John 17:23, NKJV

What moves me about the words of Jesus in this passage is His deep call for us to *cleave* to Him, to be *one* with Him, and when we respond to that call, we are reflecting the Father's answer to Christ's prayer. This is something Brother Lawrence knew. This is something that I wanted. So I set out on my own journey in an effort to discover what this Brother had found.

Brother Lawrence was born in Lorraine France to peasant parents at the turn of the seventeenth-century. It was the backdrop of power struggles and the perpetual unrest of France in his day that Nicholas Herman became Brother Lawrence. This humble Lay-monk became a shining light, which resonated with the quiet presence of Christ. Brother Lawrence understood that the holiness of God was available to everyone, no matter what his or her call, occupation, or social state in life. In fact, his life was a call to the common folk, to the butchers, bakers, and candlestick makers. He wanted them to know the depths of Christ, beyond the pew, beyond the church, in richness and in glory. Yet, he was not born with this knowledge. It was the trying times of the poverty of his youth that led him on his journey.

Poverty forced him into the army at a young age in an effort to keep a roof over his head and food in his stomach. It was during this season that Herman had a revelation. No, he wasn't overtaken by a vision, as the Apostle Paul was on the road to Damascus, yet it did have the same outcome. It was divine illumination that drove him into the arms of Christ.

In the winter of 1629, Herman stood knee-deep in the snowy landscape of a frozen winter, gazing upon a barren tree. He stood there staring at this tree, stripped of leaves with no sign of fruit and was suddenly struck by the awesome glory of God. Herman saw for the first time the hand of God's grace and the unfailing sovereignty of His divine intervention. He knew, like that tree, he himself was seemingly dead and fruitless, but God had life waiting for him, and the turn of the season would bring fullness to his soul. *"At that moment,"* he said, *'[that leafless tree] first flashed in upon my soul the fact of God, and a love for God that never after, ceased to burn."*

Not long after an injury forced him into retirement from the army. Herman was hungry for the Lord and this hunger led him on a journey that lead to the steps of the Discalced Carmelite monastery in Paris. It was there he became Brother Lawrence of the Resurrection.

At his arrival, he was assigned to the monastery kitchen. It was there that he learned the craft of a cook. It was also there that he honed his heart to honor God amidst the tiresome chores of cooking and cleaning. Subjected to the constant bidding of his superiors he developed a sense of Christ in the workplace. I suppose next to Steven in the book of Acts, Brother Lawrence was one of the first to work in what we call today "Marketplace Devotion." In his Maxims, Lawrence writes,

> *"Men invent means and methods of coming at God's love, they learn rules and set up devices to remind them of that love, and it seems like a world of trouble to bring oneself into the consciousness of God's presence. Yet it might be so simple. Is it not quicker and easier just to do our common business wholly for the love of him?"*

For Brother Lawrence, "common business," no matter how mundane or routine, was the medium of expressing and experiencing God's love. He saw the marketplace not as the task but the motivation behind the task. He did not see it as a place to gain worldly status. By doing the task and reflecting the image of Christ in the workplace, he moved upon the hearts of those around him. It was his servitude and simple humility that drew people to him. This mindset was the heartbeat of "practicing the presence of Christ." He wasn't in search for fame; he wanted everything he did in the natural to be *for* God:

> *"Nor is it needful that we should have great things to do… We can do little things for God; I turn the cake that is frying on the pan for love of him, and that done, if there is nothing else to call me, I prostrate my-*

> *self in worship before him, who has given me grace to work; afterwards I rise happier than a king. It is enough for me to pick up but a straw from the ground for the love of God."*

Brother Lawrence had found that place in his heart where the love of God made every detail of his life an act of worship, as stated in these words, *"I began to live as if there were no one save God and me in the world."* Together, God and Brother Lawrence cooked meals, stocked the pantry, washed the floors, scrubbed pots, and endured the ridicule of society.

Brother Lawrence would be the first to admit that the path to daily worship was not an easy path. He spent years disciplining his heart and mind to yield to the presence of God. In one of his letters he writes:

> *"As often as I could, I placed myself as a worshiper before him, fixing my mind upon his Holy presence, recalling it when I found it wandering from him. This proved to be an exercise frequently painful, yet I persisted through all difficulties."*

That was when he discovered the reconciliation of his soul and that in doing; he found the peace he longed for.

Brother Lawrence was a quiet man and lived in the humble state of a servant. But in that state, he was always in the presence of God, praying in all circumstances. His heart had become what had been termed at the time, *"prayerified."* For more than fifty years, this kindhearted servant was an inspiration to the friars of the monastery on the Rue Vaugirard.

During the war, he suffered an injury to his leg, which later developed into the gout. After fifteen years, the gout ended his time in the kitchen. He spent the remainder of his life as a wine merchant for the monastery. His gout finely developed into an ulcer of the leg, leaving him in intense pain. He became ill three times during the last years of his life. After he recovered from the first bout, he said to the physician, *"Doctor, your remedies have worked too well for me. You have only delayed my happiness!"* He was anxious for that glorious reunion with Christ. He, as Paul, wanted to depart and be with the Lord, which he knew was far better. Three weeks before he died, he wrote, *"Goodbye, I hope to see him soon."* Then six days before the end he wrote, *"I hope for the merciful grace of seeing him in a few days."* Brother Lawrence of the Resurrection died on February 12, 1691, at the age of seventy-seven.

Brother Lawrence teaches us, that amidst outward affairs of life and the daily grind of securing a living it is possible to cultivate a life where we can worship and participate in the glory of God within our surroundings. Every Christian, no matter what their occupation, has the ability, by the grace of God, to enjoy an ongoing fellowship with his Creator wherever he is and whatever he does. In the preface of Abbé Beaufort's edition of Lawrence's writings we read:

> *"[he was] a holy man who all his life had studied to avoid the gaze of men and whose saintliness is only fully seen now that he is dead."*

The Abbé continues:

> *"Those in the thick of the great world will learn from these Letters how greatly they deceive themselves seeking for peace and joy in the glitter of things that are seen yet temporal: those who are seeking the Highest Good will gain from this book strength to persevere in the practice of virtue."*

As you ponder the life of Brother Lawrence, listen to the humility of his heartbeat as recorded in one of his letters.

> *"Since you desire so earnestly that I should communicate to you the method by which I arrived at that habitual sense of God's presence, which our Lord, of His mercy, has been pleased to vouchsafe to me, I must tell you that it is with great difficulty that I am prevailed on by your importunities; and now I do it only upon the terms that you show my letter to nobody."*

He did not desire fame or the praise of men. His desire was to serve... and this he did to the end. There are many great culinary masters in history that one could glean. I suppose I could have talked of French politician and culinary activist Jean-Anthelme Brillat-Savarin who wrote that wonderful book on the art of dining entitled "Physiologie de Goût," translated - The Philosopher in the Kitchen in 1825. Or, perhaps I could have talked of Auguste Escoffier, Philéas Gilbert, or even Prosper Montagné.

Yet, when searching for the heartbeat of Christ in the kitchen I had to go back a few more hundred years and learn from the passions of Brother Lawrence; for he was more than a culinarian by trade... he was a light that shined into the workplace and the monastery. He spoke out the heartbeat of Jesus and it is in this heart and to this man that inspired through "the Eyes of a Chef."

CHAPTER 1

Introduction

*"The heavens declare the glory of God;
And the firmament shows His handiwork.
Day unto day utters speech,
And night unto night reveals knowledge.
There is no speech nor language
Where their voice is not heard.
Their line has gone out through all the
earth, and their words to the end of the
world.
In them He has set a tabernacle for the sun,
Which is like a bridegroom coming out of
his chamber, and rejoices like a strong man
to run its race.
Its rising is from one end of heaven,
And its circuit to the other end;
And there is nothing hidden from its heat"*

- Psalms 19:1-6

As a third generation foodie and chef, cooking has been my consuming passion as well as the source that enabled me to bring home the bacon. Whether feeding several thousand at a banquet or preparing a Christmas dinner for my family, I have always believed that the same God, who created the heavens and the earth, has also given man the ability to cook and create, and in doing so, has placed His thumbprint across the spectrum of cooking techniques and dining in general.

David understood the thumbprint of God when he proclaimed the glory of God's creation in Psalm 19 (above). I imagine David standing on his balcony on a clear and star-filled night, overlooking the city of Jerusalem, praising God. He eyes must have spanned the vastness of the city, praising God for all he had accomplished in his life, when his eyes gradually moved upwards. The beauty of God's creative hand moved him to praise and admiration. In total rapture, David began to pin this psalm after seeing the heavens in its creative splendor, possibly for the first time.

I, like David and a multitude of others throughout history, was not surprised to see the reflections of God's eternal truth woven throughout creation, and in my case, throughout the kitchen and craft of cooking. In fact, I am convinced that painted across the canvas of every occupation, task, and job, you will see the reflection of Jesus. No matter what we do, or how big or small it seems, Jesus is waiting to reveal Himself to us through every task. All we have to do is open the eyes of our hearts, eyes, and ears, and listen to the whisper of the Holy Spirit as He points to the image of Jesus within our craft.

That is what happened to me. When I stopped, and took the time to listen, I saw the image of Jesus. When I decided that this task or that chore could be so much more, I saw the reflection of Jesus appear in my cooking. When I said, "*Lord, fill my mind with your presence.*" I began to see the truth of His redeeming love fill every task I undertook. When I stopped long enough to let the voice of God fill all the gaps of my day and become one with me in the day-to-day activities of my work, I saw Him. I saw His hand painted across one end of the restaurant to the other. I saw His truth sprinkled about like seasoning on the finest of dishes. I saw His face gaze back at me from the reflection inside a stockpot of simmering amber broth. I saw Him, and in seeing Him in this way, it has helped me show Him to others.

Would it surprise you to see the gospel proclaimed in a recipe for hollandaise sauce? How about sanctification outlined in the preparation of a simple consommé? What about the concept of building your faith, do you suppose that Jesus, in His infinite wisdom, while stating, "*I am the Bread of Life*," knew the details of bread production and the effects that gluten would have on a loaf of bread? What about the whole process of dining and fellowship, is there a pattern in scripture between food, dining and spiritual truth?

The Bible opens up with the curse invading creation as a direct result of broken fellowship around the table of the Lord. Adam and Eve, consumed by the fleshly concepts of consumption, the pride of life, and the lust of the flesh, traded a table of thanksgiving and fellowship with their creator, for a table of self-centeredness. The net result left them lost, naked, and fallen from the presence of the Lord. It is no wonder when Jesus came, he proclaimed:

> *"I am the bread of life. Your fathers ate the manna in the wilderness, and are dead. This is the bread which comes down from heaven, that one may eat of it and not die. I am the living bread which came down from heaven. If anyone eats of this bread, he will live forever; and the bread that I shall give is My flesh, which I shall give for the life of the world*
>
> - John 6:48-51

It is exciting, as a chef, to see that His mission of redemption would manifest at the last supper, during the Passover feast. It is there where He proclaimed himself as the Passover lamb, whose body would be broken, flesh consumed, and blood drank, as an everlasting sign of the cross. Jesus' sacrificial death at Calvary was an act that ushered in a new creation of born again citizens, redeemed from the curse. It was the beginning of a new creation. By the time we get to the end of the book, we see the wedding feast of the Lamb and restoration of all things unto God.

Several years ago, I had the pleasure of working for Pat Robertson at CBN, as Executive Chef for the Founder's Inn and Conference Center, across from Regent University. I opened this operation for Pat as a ministry unto the Lord. That season in my life was a turning point for me. The Lord began showing me incredible parables and symbolism scattered across the landscape of cooking. This season dramatically changed how I look at cooking and the culinary arts. It was during that time, that the Lord placed in my heart the desire to write a book.

My prayer is that, as you read this book, your soul will ignite with a greater hunger to pursue, take, and eat of our Lord and Savior Jesus Christ. I pray that no matter what your profession, you would invite the Holy Spirit into your day-to-day tasks and let Jesus reveal himself in every detail of your work so you will join the ranks of Brother Lawrence, a cook for Christ, and participate in the "*Practice of the Presence of God.*"

CHAPTER 2

The Parable of the Sower

As seen through my father's garden

"A sower went out to sow his seed. And as he sowed, some fell by the wayside; and it was trampled down, and the birds of the air devoured it. Some fell on rock; and as soon as it sprang up, it withered away because it lacked moisture. And some fell among thorns, and the thorns sprang up with it and choked it. But others fell on good ground, sprang up, and yielded a crop a hundredfold." When He had said these things He cried, "He who has ears to hear, let him hear"

- Luke 8:5-8

My dad was an outstanding cook. He was a restaurant man, working in every aspect of the industry. In the 50s he owned and operated his own place. He had a café in a bowling alley during the 60s. In his later years he tended and managed a California bar and BBQ joint. He was a great bartender, but his true love was cooking and gardening. He was not a gourmet's cook but a comfort cook, a good old savory cook. His food was well spiced and aromatic. His style was a blend of the ethnic flavors of Mexico and Asia – all bound together on a foundation of California comfort cooking. Dad would spend all day in the kitchen. His one-pot meals would take hours to cook until they tasted the way he wanted. It was all about flavor. He cooked the kind of food that dances upon the tongues of its eaters. It is the kind of food that tastes much better in a crowded kitchen than in an empty one.

When you entered into our house, you knew that the kitchen was the place to hangout. When you nudged your way past my Uncle Bud's over-sized beer-belly, and hopped past my aunt's rightly sized feet, you discover it's standing-room-only and the one place left to stand was in the hallway, outside the kitchen. That's where the pleasure of family and the table would come alive. There I was, standing with my head halfway cocked into the kitchen, trying to see if I missed any excitement. That was the kitchen in my home. It was the center of all our family gatherings.

Typically, the staples found at our table consisted of a big, giant, humongous pot of chili, fresh crispy-fried tortilla chips, Southern fried chicken gizzards, livers, and hearts, and a big galvanized tub of hot steaming tamales, all of which were snacks until dinner was ready. The aroma used to fill the house. I would answer the door and get that all-too-common-response "Just point me in the direction of Libby's (my dad) chili." It was different then.

I remember standing at the kitchen window, eating soft corn tortilla tacos and juggling very hot... sizzling-hot... just-out-of-the-cast-iron-skillet hot... fried chicken gizzards in my hand while watching our jet-black cat Kiki, prowl around the backyard lurking for birds and bugs to prey upon. I would stand there wondering what it would be like to play in that yard like our cat. My dad had a great yard. It was the best yard in the neighborhood. His garden and his kitchen, the two were so closely woven in my memory, it's a wonder I never became a gardener. To a child, it was a forest of exotic plants, and to our cat, it was like living in the Garden of Eden.

One day, while staring out the window, I saw Kiki fly by... I mean fly... ten or twelve feet off the ground... and in the air. I didn't see where she started and I didn't see where she landed... but I did see her fly. I ran out the back door and there she was, as proud as can be, standing with a bird tucked between her teeth. She walked up to my Dad, my brother Paul, and myself, and laid that bird at our feet. I didn't know what to do. I was speechless. I guess my dad saw the confused look on my face and said that Kiki was just trying to show us her gratitude - how much she loved us. "Its' in their nature," he said. I will never forget that day. We gave the bird a proper burial and headed about our day. I even think we bragged about it to our friends, on what a mighty bird-hunter Kiki was.

Well, several years ago I had the back aching - weed pulling – bushwhacking - pleasure of going back and working in my father's garden. Boy, do I mean work, sweat-of-the-brow kind of work. Oh, I've known the meaning sweat and hard work all my life, but it was usually behind a hot stove, feeding people. This back-bending weed-pulling work had given me a whole new perspective for the vegetables I cook. Typically, working in my father's garden, consisted of a little weeding and a little watering, but not this time. Its not that my father didn't know how to garden, on the contrary, he was a true gardener in the purist sense of the term.

My Dad was a man of many passions: cooking, science, politics, medicine, and nature, but his love for his garden was the one constant that endured his eighty-six years of life. I am still dumbfounded at the things he could do with plants. As a child, I remember wandering around the garden asking him questions about all the plants. It was like living in a park, all the vines, flowers, cactus, and stuff. My all time favorite plant had to be the fern. Dad would always answer my questions with an excited, childlike smile, as if I had touched on a topic of deep affection.

With a glimmer in his eyes, starting with their common names, and ending with their true name, their Latin name, their name according to Hortus Americanus, my father would point out all the plants. At that moment, in the height of his excitement, he would show me his special creations, the ones he made with grafts and cuttings.

Though I have long forgotten the scientific names, I still remember a few with their common name... the "mother leaf fern," the "Boston fern," (not a fern) and the "squirrel's foot" fern. The greatest of the fern clan had to be the "staghorn fern." The staghorn is a majestic antler-looking fern. My Dad used to attach these wonderful ferns to old pieces of driftwood, tree stumps, or wire baskets, and tightly pack them with Peat moss and fertilize them with banana peels. I was amazed at how he got them to grow. I was sure it had to be the Peat moss and the banana peels. I mean what a great word... "Peat moss" sounds magical, and banana peels – who would have thought? Yes, my father had the soul of a true Gardner... a Gardner with a magnificent mind and soiled hands that have withstood the test of time.

Nevertheless, his age had caught up with him. Time had decided to settle in on this once "sharp as a tack" mind. Remembering was not as easy as it once was. Life was starting to slow down. My father spent his final days taking care of his dear friend and companion Margaret who, after an intense struggle with osteosclerosis, was bed ridden with a broken hip. Between his dementia and talking care of his dear friend, his garden had taken on a life of its own. This once stately garden had decided to invade, not only every square foot of his trailer space, but his neighbor's space as well.

So there I was, with my wife, a chef by trade, cutting my way through my father's yard. Inch by inch, we walked through Dad's yard, taking territory, as if we was cutting our way through the Amazon. The oddity is... the only thing I know about gardening were the images I captured when I was a child, and of course, the abundance of produce I have sliced and diced over the last thirty plus years. Yet, I enjoyed that time in my father's garden, over-grown and out-of-control as it was.

A garden is a splendid place. It has a powerful tranquility about it. It will tame and quiet the most restless soul. It quieted me; I had come to see why my father was drawn to a life in the garden. The garden is a sanctuary. It is a place of prayer, peace, and meditation. A place occupied by the quietness of the wind, the fragrance of the soil, and the music of the birds and the wind chimes. I love it very much.

As I dipped my hands in the soil and rubbed the clumps of dirt between my fingers, my mind was filled with images. I pictured God walking in the garden in the cool of the day. I wondered how incredibly beautiful Eden must have been. Adam must have been dumbfounded, as he looked at all the glorious beauty... so fresh and new.... Then all of a sudden, my mind wondered back to the weed pulling task-at-hand. It wasn't long again before I would find myself wandering off again at the movement of a white butterfly floating by dancing from flower to flower. That is the magic of a garden, its incredible ability to cause you to ponder and reflect on life and its incredible eco-system. With every ache in my body, I had discovered a new secret in the Garden, the depths of prayer, and intersession.

One afternoon, while pulling out old pots of dead and dying plants that had fallen behind an old table I came across the most stubborn pot I had ever seen. Normally, when I worked with pots like this I try to save the soil. Most of the time, it is done with ease; the soil pops out and simply breaks apart to be used later for re-potting. This one though, had me going. It was stuck, hard as a rock and dry as a bone. I worked on that pot for a good fifteen minutes before getting that clump of dirt out.

While I was hitting that clump with a hammer trying to break it apart the Lord brought back to my mind a vision he gave me some 15 years earlier.

I was a new Christian and was not as grounded in the word or in my walk, as I should have been. I was Executive Chef for a five star resort in the Palm Springs area and was ambitious with my career. I had got in a squabble with my wife earlier that day. For the life of me, I couldn't tell you what it was about, but by the end of the day I was feeling rotten. I remember driving along the mountain range from Rancho Mirage towards Palm Springs mumbling to myself and feeling distant from the Lord. He really dislikes it when we squabble. I felt disqualified to do anything for God. I had not yet learned that its' all Him. While driving I had made this statement in my mind - "**I feel like dirt!**" though I think it was more like a groan.

All of a sudden, at that very moment, I saw this picture, an image that filled my mind like watching a panorama movie. It was clear and overwhelming, I was taken back. In this vision, I saw Jesus dressed as a farmer. He was standing tall and firm with a pitchfork in His hand. His hair was blowing in the wind and behind Him; the sun was golden as if it had just risen. He reached down and grabbed a handful of dirt, and with the gracefulness of an Olympic Gardener, he extended His arm outward and slowly spun around blowing on His hand, causing the dirt to fly outwards as a gardener sowing seeds, He was spraying them everywhere. As the dirt hit the ground crops began to sprout up. Then I heard the voice of the Lord say...

"Boy, what I could do with dirt!"

At that moment, I began to cry as the Spirit of God touched me on my way home. Jesus had met me where I was. He heard my pain and confusion and He showed up with the peace, power, and presence of the God I love. I knew it was all Him. I knew I was mere dirt in the Master's hands and the Master likes it that way.

Well, there I was 15 years later... bent over a big plastic bucket with an old, hard clump of dirt in my hands. Now, instead of the hammer that I was using a few seconds earlier to break apart that clump of dirt, the dirt crumbled between my fingers. The breaking point was the gentle wind of God's Spirit combined with the tears that were running down my checks as Jesus reminded me how much He loved me and how long He has worked to break up the soil of my own life and in my own heart. I began to understand the depth of his love for us, and the perseverance towards us all, in preparing a heart of soil that is fit for a gardeners' planting. Of course, it is painted throughout the scriptures that way.

It is remarkable to me that in the scriptures gardening and cooking (or eating), are so closely related, more so food than gardens. I guess that is due to our fallen nature to be consumers more than laborers. Yet in every major event, you will see these two in close proximity. Take for example the following:

- The creation of man took place in the Garden of Eden; Sin entered in at the consumption of the forbidden fruit in the garden.

- Christ's glorious prayer prior to His betrayal and journey to the cross took place in the garden of Gethsemane; His final fellowship with His disciples, prior to His betrayal and journey to the cross, happened during Passover, at the last supper.

- Jesus' burial and resurrection took place in a garden; our resurrected fellowship with Him, in heaven will take place at the wedding supper of the lamb.

God must love to garden. I dare say He enjoys it almost as much as cooking and fellowship at the table. See why the garden is the perfect picture of everything Christ does in our lives. Look at the analogy of sowing and reaping. It is a picture of God planting the seed of His Word into the hearts of men and reaping a harvest of born-again children.

Or, consider the picture of a gardener pruning his garden. It is the perfect figure of God's work and commitment in our lives to bring about change and transformation. It is also His transforming work in which the church becomes the bride... a bride without spot or blemish, weed or thistle, however, the garden is not the end in and of itself.

The garden is the process. The garden is the place of preparation. The garden is the place in which the Kingdom of God becomes complete. The garden is the place in which all those, whose names are written in the Lamb's book of life, have been accounted for and are ready to enter into His glory. The garden is the church age in which He prepares His new creation for the coming of the New Jerusalem, the kingdom of God, here on earth as it is in heaven. If the garden is the preparation – then the end is the completed meal.

The end is a new beginning... the beginning of a new creation, - celebrated at the wedding feast of the Lamb. There will be no more sowing, no more reaping... a season of fellowship that is face to face with the Lord our God. I have always wondered what is going to be on the menu that day.

I have often imagined how blessed it would be to assist our Master Chef and Lord with the cooking of that meal. Wouldn't be wonderful to stand side-by-side with the greatest of all cooks and prepare a manna soufflé or possibly warm caramel pecan manna-bread-pudding? What a joy that day would be! Oh well, for now I'll keep on roasting and grilling my way into the hearts of those around me as I learn the depths and the ways of the Master Gardener... until the day I hear the voice of the bridegroom say... "Come."

One thing I've learned in my father's garden is a how tenacious weed and root systems can be. They are extremely powerful. They search out every inch of exposed soil and dive deeply into it. My Dad had this one plant, I am not sure what it is called, some kind of groundcover spider plant, it has these long, soft slender green leaves and several very long stems that shoot out of the center of it. At the end of each steam is a small, miniature version of the plant with a cluster of its exposed root system. The root cluster is whitish translucent and appears to house water. When this plant is hanging in a basket from a well-groomed garden, it is quite pretty.

On the other hand, if the garden goes untreated this little plant will start to take over the entire yard, shooting out cluster after cluster and growing on anything and everything it lands on. That was one of the major challenges I faced when bringing order to my Dads' overlooked garden. In thinking about it, the parallel of the foliage in our own lives is all too clear.

We must look at our lives as a prudent Gardener. We must learn to yield up every plant and growth we have collected throughout our lives and give it up to the Lord. We must nurture our garden; keeping it well watered and safe from diseases and pests that destroy what God is planting in our lives.

If you are in a place like the hardened soil of a heart not plowed, or in a place of plowing and planting the garden of your own life, or better still, in that place of sowing seed and planting a harvest of souls for the Kingdom of God, learn from my Father's Garden. Learn to weed and to water. Learn when to plant and when to harvest. Learn when to cut away and trim back. Learn to smell the soil with your bare hands and come to know the value and richness that is within. Then you will meet the Lord in the air and your soil stained hands will be lifted up in worship to our King, but to the Father, your hands will be as white as snow.

My father went to be with the Lord in January of 2004 – and I know that he is happily working in the Master's garden. I dedicate this life lesson to my Dad.

CHAPTER 3

A Community of Believers

As seen through a garden salad

"To make a good salad is to be a brilliant diplomatist – the problem is entirely the same in both cases. To know how much oil one must mix with one's vinegar."

- Oscar Wilde

"Two heads are better than one."

- John Heywood

"For as the body is one and has many members, but all the members of that one body, being many, are one body, so also is Christ"

- 1 Corinthians 12:6

William Shakespeare said, - *"My salad days, when I was green in judgment,"* referring to a time of youthful innocence and inexperience. We all know those days and I suppose some of us are still having them. Now, in this modern, less poetic time of society, salad days mean something entirely different. Salad days are healthy, flag waving, consumption days. The salad itself has taken on a completely new identity compared to the humble role it once played at the beginning of the meal, to us Americans, or after the main course, to those from Europe, specifically France.

Today, often the salad is center stage - served as the main course, or for better or worse, it becomes a banqueting feast unto itself. The infamous salad bar, a never-ending trip to the greens machine, that once adorned virtually every casual restaurant for the last forty years, causing us to truly veg-out like cattle, grazing and parading our way around a nearby restaurant only to be enhanced by its' dear friend the potato bar.

Salads come in all shapes and sizes. They appear on the menu in so many different guises. Today's chef has embraced salads with such enthusiasm and speed you would think they had invented it. History tells us that the ancient Greeks and Romans enjoyed a wonderful salad known as herba salata, made of herbs and lettuces dipped in fresh vinegar and resting in a small pool of extra virgin olive oil. Ummm... sounds yummy.

One of the main ingredients in the typical garden salad is lettuce. What a wonderful word - the word "lettuce" is. It is almost a proclamation. It beckons all its comrades to jump into the salad bowl and create something grand. It is a command, a call to action - a culinary trumpet if you will. Lettuce is the pastor, the preacher, the evangelist of a Holy community that calls for oneness and family. You almost hear it say... Come... Enter In... Pursue your heart's desires... Join the team for together we can do amazing things.... Lettuce do this... Lettuce do that... Lettuce achieve the imposable... *Lettuce serve the Lord with all our hearts, and core, and outer leaves too.*

I love that little poem, written by someone named Anonymous, a famous writer whose works have appeared everywhere....

> *"Lettuce entertain you, Lettuce make you smile,*
>
> *Lettuce make a salad, the calories are valid,*
>
> *To put your bod in style."*
>
> - Anonymous

Salads are the ideal community. A combination of all these fantastic, friendly ingredients, whether hot or cold, spicy or fruity, light or crisp, combining themselves with such ease that they become one. Yet each ingredient maintains its own individual flavor, texture, and aroma. They all are one, but extremely individualized in the role they play in the salad. We could learn a lot from salad. If only the church would come together as easily as the salad. No instead, we side on our varieties – the Romaine sits with the Romaine and the Iceberg worships with the Iceberg.

How hard it is for us to come together, let alone, not be threatened by the gifting and contribution of another. We want center stage. We want to be the main course - the center of the plate. The sad thing is, often in our minds there has not, nor will not be another course, we are the end-all to end all courses. We block out the previous and out-perform those who come after us, not realizing that the grand plan of a seven-course dinner is the satisfaction and fullness at the end of the meal.

Every course is vital to the program – from the amuse gueule or the simple appetizer to the grand soufflé or the cheese & fruit course, and the only one that is going to take a bow at this dinner is the Master Chef, Jesus Christ, who gave His life to prepare this dinner. He has sent a letter to each of the courses, reminding them of their place in the meal – you can read them in the book of Revelation, chapters two and three. They are called "*the seven letters to the seven churches,*" but I will refer to them as - a message to the seven heads of lettuce – facing the salad bowl of eternity. I do not want to ramble on so – lettuce continue….

One day I was telling my wife, about how beautiful I thought salads were and lettuce in particular. I told her that lettuce was in the daisy family (Lactuca sativa). Jan loves daisies. She loves the daisy's sense of freedom - how they grow so wild and free. They have an earthy elegance about them. She loves their colors and the simplicity of their petals. They have a circular golden radiance about them like nature's crown or the bright innocent eyes of a child standing in a field of green. Though she laughs at my analogous way of looking at life, she really does enjoy listening to me.

That night we made ourselves a wonderful salad, sat on the sofa, under a warm cuddly blanket and watched a movie. If you and your wife are ever having one of those nights were you can't think of anything to do, fire up Netflix or iTunes and watch an old heart warming movie. Then make yourselves an exciting salad together. Place your salad in a big wooden bowl, cuddle under an old warm blanket, and enjoy your salad together. You will thank me in doing so. We did just that and we are glad we did, Honest!

Rarely, does one find a movie that demands to be viewed a second, or even, a third time. The film we selected was one just like that. It was that 1989 classic, "Driving Miss Daisy." It is, without a doubt, one of those "rent-me-again" movies. For those who do not remember, it is a film of deep affection, patience, friendship, and commitment. It is a movie about change, changes in culture, changes in relationship, and changes in the lives and minds of its characters as they advance into old age. It moves from distrust to long-lasting friendship. The movie tells the story of two very different people, Miss Daisy Werthan, a proud stubborn Southern lady in Georgia, and Hoke Colburn, her black chauffeur.

The movie spans a quarter century in the lives of its two characters, from 1948, when Miss Daisy's son decides it is time she stops driving herself and employees a chauffeur, to 1973, when two old people acknowledge the bond that has grown between them. It is an enormously subtle film. If you watch this movie closely, you will notice the quiet messages displayed in the simple tone of voice or the look in an eye. Those moments can be the most important moments in a scene. After being bombarded with so many movies that are driven and fueled by shallow violence it is refreshing to take in a movie that explores the depth of the human heart. Who else better to play those roles than the outstanding actor Morgan Freeman, as Hoke, and the dear, then 80 year old Jessica Tandy as Miss Daisy, who passed away in 1995.

I must confess when I rented this film it was the title that drew me, and not my recollection of what the movie was about. The key words in the title were "Daisy" and "Driving." I had been working on this chapter and was having a healthy discussion with Jan about lettuce when – there I was standing in the isle staring at that DVD when a question popped in my head, "What's driving Miss Daisy?" It was perfect... the target topic for this chapter. I will explain.

Several years ago, I was consulting for a facility in the South. My objective was to assess their food operations and come up with a plan to take their dining program to the next level. During this process, we discovered a real need for an additional "a la carte" restaurant. The

"Wagon Wheel Café" was conceived and the building process commenced. During the opening of this restaurant, I had a dishwasher; I will call him John, who was in his late thirties. He was confused about life and struggling in his marriage. John was a hard worker who loved to talk, and more, he loved to complain.

One day while preparing for lunch, I asked John to clean several heads of radicchio, leaving the outer leaves whole and intact that way I could use them later. Radicchio resembles a small red cabbage. Its leaves are bright to dark purplish pink and extremely attractive. It is popular braised or grilled and served as a vegetable side dish. This is a European custom but American's have a hard time with grilled lettuce. It is also well suited for cold salads, but it has a bitter flavor and should be used sparingly and mixed with other greens. Its outer leaves make wonderful cups when separated to hold other ingredients or composed salads, and that is what I had planned to do with those leaves.

Well that was John's task. Since John had been helping the Garde Manger (cold food production chef) the previous day I assumed John had been trained in this task. To my surprise, he had not. After listening to John complain about his wife for about the tenth time, I turned and saw John still wrestling at the sink with his first head of radicchio, mumbling, as he struggled to separate each leaf and keep them whole.

As he butchered that poor little head of expensive lettuce, I heard him say, *"Why doesn't she ever listen to me? ...What's wrong with her, I feel like I am talking to a wall! ...Why can't she see? ...She acts as if I'm not even here! ...Divorce... what's wrong with her?"*

At that moment, while I was observing, John shred to pieces that poor little head, I heard that small still voice, a prompting of the Holy Spirit, which said,

>*"That's what he is doing to his wife."*

I prayed, "What Lord?"

He said,

>*"He is tearing her apart, ripping the leaves of her life into pieces, trying to get through and without me... its' destructive."*

I suddenly understood what the Lord was saying. John's wife was like that head of radicchio, John did not know how to reach her and God was on the move desiring to touch both John and his wife.

I stopped in my tracks and asked the Lord what I should do. The Spirit said,

>*"Tell him."*

Well that is exactly what I was going to do and if I got it wrong or missed-the-mark in this analogous dialog, at least I could save that delicate head of radicchio, so step out I did.

When I approached John, I placed my hand on his shoulder and said, *"Here, let me help you with that."* I looked in his eyes and asked him if he was ok.

John started in... frustrated and confused, complaining about his wife again. I looked at John and told him that Jesus can heal this situation, that he would repair the brokenness of his marriage.

I said,

> *"John, I believe God has shown me that what you are doing to your wife is the same thing you are doing to that head of radicchio. John, you are tearing her apart. Verbally, trying to rip those leaves off hoping she will hear you."* I took the pairing knife and radicchio from his hand and set them aside.
>
> *"John, Jesus is gentle. He knows how to reach the deepest area of our lives and bring light where there once was only darkness."* I told John, *"People are like heads of lettuce, all kinds of lettuce, each different and unique in its own way.*
>
> *Take, for example, a head of iceberg. When you clean iceberg, after removing the old dark outer leaves, if you take the head in your hand and slam the core down on the counter, the core pops right out and the head easily comes apart in your hand. I was, before I became a Christian, and God*

> *had to pick me up by the head and slam me down on the counter. Kind of like the old 2 x 4 smacked upside an old stubborn donkey's head.*
>
> *It hurt, but it worked and now I am saved. Some people are heads of Romaine, tall and steadfast, but their heads are exposed to all kinds of debris and dirt, so washing between the leaves is crucial in dealing with that lettuce variety. Some folks are curly red or green leaf lettuce; they look beautiful with their ruffled edges and two tone colors. One problem though, they are exposed to the outer elements like Romaine, but due to the frailty of their leaves they, not only have a tendency to get dirty, but they also burse and rot easily and the need for even extra care is twice as important. Do you understand what I am driving at?"*

John was starting to get it.

"*John,*" I said,

> "*Your wife is a head of radicchio. What you are doing to that head right now is tearing it apart and actually damaging the head, causing it to be worse off than if you never touched it at all.*"

I saw God touching John's heart at that moment and I watched as tears welled up in his eyes.

> "John, look. It is easy when you know how and Jesus is the how. Jesus always starts with us. He always likes to work in an area that has been cleaned and prepped for production. That process is repentance, confession, forgiveness, and salvation. Just like preparing salad, it is important that you have a clean, neat, and orderly workspace,"

I said, as I moved crates, containers and other such kitchen goodies from his prep sink and work area.

I asked John if he had a close relationship with the Lord. John had not. I prayed with John and led him through the sinner's prayer. God was touching John in a special way and I was going along for the ride.

I said,

> "John, just like the second step in making salad, when you soak the lettuce in icy cold water, Jesus wants to fill us with the Holy Spirit, giving us the power and refreshing us to do His will. He fills us with living water. See what I mean."

I filled one sink with icy cold water.

I continued,

> "The reason for this is three fold... just as the ribs of a head of lettuce absorbs the water and help keep it fresh so your spirit

> *absorbs the Spirit of His presence.... Secondly, the cold water, like the Holy Spirit, will crisp the leaves and firm up their texture, likewise, firming you up and giving you a new vibrancy.... Thirdly, the water is the final stage in cleaning the leaves before it is served to others. We constantly need the filling and refreshing of the Holy Spirit in our lives if we are going to touch the lives of others."*

I asked John if I could pray for him to receive the Holy Spirit and you can guess the outcome. John was bubbling over with the Holy Spirit. I couldn't believe my eyes. All I needed to do was speak to John about the dynamics of radicchio, point him in the direction of a good counselor, and pray for him and his wife.

I reached down and grabbed a head of radicchio, took a pairing knife, removed the core. Now this is an important step... I placed the head under slow running cold water. As the head filled up with water, the leaves fell right into my hands. John had been pulling at the leaves and tearing them apart. Radicchio is a very tight, bitter, head of lettuce. I explained to John how Jesus, over time would slowly fill his wife, like the cool running water, with his presence and heal their marriage. None of John's wrestling would have accomplished anything. I told him,

> *"It was that slow drizzle of cold water that eased its way between the leaves, filling all the gaps, and loosing each leaf, one at a*

> *time, till they all came apart, that got the job done. Give Jesus the opportunity to pour out His life into you and your wife – only then will you see real healing."*

John got-it and began to cry, thanking me for my help. I told John, don't thank me, give your thanks to Jesus, I was about to ring your neck for the way you were ripping that head apart – until God opened my heart and eyes to your situation. The Spirit of God was touching him and opening his eyes as well to his abrasive approach.

John looked at me and asked what he should do.

"*For starters,*" I told him, *"we needed to pray and see if we can get you two into counseling."*

As John and I prayed, our heads bowed at that pantry sink, God had started the healing process.

Periodically, throughout the day, I would explain to John how Jesus was the only one that can remove the core in her life. That he must go, humbly, and ask for forgiveness from his wife for all that he has done wrong. I told John that when she forgives you, that will only be the beginning, like removing the core out of that head of radicchio.

Later on that night I began to think about lettuce, all the wonderful varieties, each with their own flavor, texture, and taste. I thought it wonderful how in describing lettuce we refer to them as "**heads**" of lettuce. Now as I stood looking at that title "Driving Miss Daisy" and thinking about the question of "What's driving Miss Daisy?" I understood that people, like heads of lettuce, come in many varieties. Each person or personality type is parallel to the varieties found in this edible daisy family.

Within each lettuce type are several varieties that offer their own unique traits, shapes, flavors, and methods of preparation. Each, parallel to the human persona it is striking. Today, I have a completely new perspective on lettuce. Each variety different yet all are called to hop into the salad bowl and take their position in the kingdom of God.

The funny thing is that now, when I look at people I ask the question, "*What's driving Miss Daisy?*" The answer usually comes in the form of a picture of some kind of lettuce.... Only after knowing who and what I am dealing with, am I able to be effective in ministering to their needs. God is preparing a banquet and the salad is the main course. Lets do all we can and pull our heads together, jump in the bowl, and get on with the task of making a great salad to serve a hungry dying world. That is what being a member of the body of Christ is all about!

CHAPTER 4

Salvation

As seen through a Hollandaise sauce

"A hen is only an egg's way of making another egg."

- Samuel Butler

"You can't make an omelet without breaking eggs."

- French proverb

"When Jesus Christ shed his blood on the cross, it was not the blood of a martyr; or the blood of one man for another; it was the life of God poured out to redeem the world."

- Oswald Chambers (1874–1917)

Why is it that every restaurant in town is packed with a twenty-minute wait at 1:00 PM on a Sunday afternoon? It seems that the magical hours between 11:00 and 1:00 are the most grueling hours for cooks in restaurants. In ala carte restaurants, you have changed over all your production from breakfast to lunch and the morning cooks are getting ready to head home at 1:00.

Most of the time, all the breakfast mise en place has disappeared, the ingredients for omelets, the diced ham, diced tomatoes and grated cheese. The eggs are back in the walk-in. The hash browns are frozen and burger orders are starting to come in. It never fails, on Sunday everyone wants breakfast. You inevitability scramble around the kitchen trying to set up for breakfast at the last minute, even though you know that this is going to happen 52 weeks a year.

The reason you're busy is understandable, - HUNGER PAINS! It's the same every Sunday. I should know. I have spent the last 35 years feeding those hunger pains. Not my own mind you, but everyone else's. For me personally, breakfast consists of a giant cup of coffee. I usually don't grab a bite to eat until around 3:00 PM.

In the old days my Sunday mornings usually went like this: I would get up at 5:00 am and call the kitchen to make sure the morning crew had arrived on time. The weekends are about a 50/50 hit or miss due to the intense desire for foodies to go out and party after work. After I received the starting lineup I would rush in to work, walk the café to ensure everything was going well, then head to the main kitchen and begin to set up for Sunday Brunch. If I am lucky, they pulled the ice carving out of the freezer to temper. If I am really lucky, they didn't break it on the way out of the freezer. I can't tell you how many times in the last 35 years I have had to grab my chain saw and carve out an ice carving only to get it up minutes before we were ready to open. My unsung heroes did it again, we're ready to roll, its 10:00 AM, brunch was now open; and the crowds were ready to come in.

You can almost hear their growling stomachs. They shoot up from their tables and spread out like locust on a field of wheat. 25% would head to the carving and omelet station, 25% to the waffle station, and 25% to the salad and fruit tables. The rest make their way to the hot food line ready to feast on hand-rolled cheese blintzes with fresh raspberries and almond-butter sauce, or grilled grouper laced with mango salsa. One of the more popular items on the hot line was the classic Eggs Benedict graced with a delightful hollandaise sauce. That is where my wife would head. She loves Eggs Benedict.

On the other hand, my cooks despised Hollandaise. Not the sauce really, just the hurdles they overcome in its' preparation. The two culprits found in Eggs Benedict are poached eggs and Hollandaise sauce! Now, I am not so interested in poached eggs in this chapter, and I had trained my cooks on the art of poaching then submerging the eggs in ice water for later use, so the poaching of eggs were not the issue. What I want to focus on is making Hollandaise sauce, or in a broader sense – emulsified sauces.

Within Hollandaise sauce there is a principle and technique that many young cooks fail to grasp or struggle to master. Yet, its' that technique and principle that excites me the most about hollandaise sauce, and all emulsified sauces. Within the building blocks of a hollandaise a picture unfolds that gives you a glimpse into the mystery of the universe. In it you will see the symbolism of salvation through the death and resurrection of our Lord and Savior Jesus Christ.

Let me explain. Hollandaise is an emulsion sauce. An emulsion is formed when one substance is suspended in another. In this case, clarified butter (oil) is suspended in water. The need for an emulsion arises when two or more ingredients repel each other and chemically will not mix. In the case of a hollandaise sauce, the two unequally yoked items are the acids, water (cider vinegar and lemon juice) and the oil (clarified butter). We all know oil and water do not mix; they need a stabilizer – an emulsifier.

What is an Emulsifier?

An emulsifier is the agent that brings two liquids that are incapable. They will not mix together to form a single homogeneous substance, or are not emulsified. Examples of emulsions include crude oil, butter and margarine, hand lotion, mayonnaise, hollandaise, the photosensitive side of film stock, and cutting fluid for metalworking. Emulsification is the process by which emulsions are prepared.

Emulsions tend to have a cloudy appearance, because a boundary between oil and water, called an interface, that scatters light that passes through the emulsion. Emulsions can be stable or unstable. Simple vinaigrette is an unstable emulsion and has to be shaken continuously or will quickly separate.

An emulsifier, or emulgent, is a substance that stabilizes an emulsion. Examples of emulsifiers in the kitchen include egg yolks, mustard, glucose, and nuts. Whether an emulsion turns into a water-in-oil emulsion or an oil-in-water emulsion depends upon the volume fraction of both phases and on the type of emulsifier. Emulsifiers and emulsifying particles tend to promote dispersion of the phase in which they do not dissolve well. For example, proteins dissolve better in water than in oil and tend to form oil-in-water emulsions (that is they promote the dispersion of oil droplets throughout a continuous phase of water).

Another important characteristic of an emulsion is the requirement of energy in its formation. Anyone that has made a large batch of hollandaise will attest to a sore arm the next day - part of the price to be paid in its' preparation. It's this agitation, tension, and constant whipping that enables the emulsifiers within the egg yolk (lecithin) to bring together the acids (water) and the oil (butter) in the formation of the sauce.

The molecular structure of compounds within the yolk, such as lecithin and cholesterol are emulsifiers. In the later, cholesterol stabilizes water-in-oil emulsions for sauces such as mayonnaise. Hollandaise, on the other hand uses lecithin, which has a larger water-soluble head and stabilizes oil-in-water emulsions. You get the picture.

Now let's take a deeper look at the preparation of this sauce starting with the problem – *incompatibility!* As I stated earlier, oil and water do not mix. A dilemma that is very parallel to the problem that has plagued all of creation since the fall of man in the Garden of Eden. *It is the curse, eternal separation between God and humanity.*

Because of the curse humanity was expelled from the presence of God, unable to freely be united with Him. An eternal void entered into the heart of man. God and humanity had become two unequally yoked entities, two substances that repelled each other. Like the acid and oil in our Hollandaise, they were forever separated until the emulsification had taken place. There was a need for a mediator, an emulsifier to unite God and man.

Even the prophets of old cried out for a solution to this dilemma. To quote Isaiah:

> *"Oh, that You would rend the heavens!*
>
> *That You would come down!*

> *That the mountains might shake at Your presence—"*

- Isaiah 64: 1

Who is this great emulsifier that would unite mankind with God? The parabolic answer in our recipe is the *egg yolk*. An egg is a remarkable thing. The eggs botanical counterparts are seeds. Seeds are the most nutritious food on earth, not to mention their place in the first promise of redemption found in scripture. In God's judgment upon the serpent, he said,

> *"And I will put enmity*
>
> *Between you and the woman,*
>
> *And between your seed and her Seed;*
>
> *He shall bruise your head,*
>
> *And you shall bruise His heel"*

- Gen. 3:15

From the Scriptures we know that Jesus is the seed of the woman and that He crushed the head of satan at Calvary. Hopefully, you are starting to see a parabolic picture begin to form.

The Process

In its' simplest definition the egg is composed of three parts, the white (albumen), the yolk, and the shell. In our recipe the yolk must be separated from its' other two components. I compare the egg in this analogy to the Godhead and the yolk to the Son of God. This is the incarnation.

In the first step, the shell is cracked and broken open and the yolk is pulled away from its' rightful place. The yolk is tossed into a cold stainless steal bowl. Lonely and isolated, the yolk has one mission in mind to unite that, which chemically cannot be mixed, our sinful nature with a Holy God. In order to do this, the yolks have to endure terrible suffering.

The yolks are placed in a stainless steal bowl over hot simmering water. Vinegar (or lemon juice) is added to the yolks. The yolks are then beaten with a wire whip, causing the flesh of the yolks to be broken. The heat of the water intensifies and the yolks begin to cook under turbulence and torture, as the whip moves, until there is no life left in the yolks.

Then, at just the right moment, the bowl is removed from the boiling water and warm butter (the oil of God) is slowly whisked in. Suddenly, as if by some miracle, an emulsion begins to take place. The yolks, that were once dead, come back to life. The acidic mixture that was once separated from the presence of the oil is now united by the work of the mediator, the yolks (Jesus).

It was the process of agitation and tension (beaten and crucified) that enabled the emulsification to take place. When the oil of God is fully incorporated into the cooked mixture, the sauce is complete and He has risen - It is finished!

> *"For there is one God and one Mediator between God and men, the Man Christ Jesus, who gave Himself a ransom for all, to be testified in due time,"*
>
> - 1 Timothy 2:5, 6

All around us, the Lord is proclaiming His eternal truth. His desire is that all would come to the saving knowledge of faith in Him. Look around you. Everywhere you turn the Spirit is pointing you to Jesus, all you have to do is listen. Look around, milk, cream, butter, mayonnaise, cosmetic creams, floor and furniture waxes, some paints, asphalt, and even crude oil, are all emulsions symbolically pointing to Christ. As you look around the world or in your workplace – what do you see? I challenge you... if you look hard, enough you will see the Holy Spirit prompting you to look deeper – and see the salvation of the Lord.

> *"After this, Jesus, knowing that all things were now accomplished, that the Scripture might be fulfilled, said, " I thirst!" Now a vessel full of sour wine was sitting there; and they filled a sponge with sour wine, put it on hyssop, and put it to His mouth. So when Jesus had received the sour wine,*

> *He said, " It is finished!" And bowing His head, He gave up His spirit"*
>
> - John 19:28-30

If you don't know Jesus and the power of His saving grace, I encourage you to let Him into your life. Give Jesus a chance. He is more than able to meet you where you are and forgive you of all your sins. You see, relationship with God can only happen under the process of emulsification. Jesus is that emulsifier. His blood is the emulsifier. We cannot help our condition. Just as h2o based substances (water, acids, vinegars) cannot unite with oil (they repel), so likewise humanity is with God. Nevertheless, there is an answer to this dilemma. Much like the separation of the yolk from the egg Jesus left his home as God in heaven and came down to earth in the form of a man. Jesus gathered all the sins of humanity, past, present, and future, and placed them upon His self. He was crucified on a cross as judgment for those sins. Jesus arose from the dead and in doing so conquered sin and death. Today, He sits at the right hand of the Father ready to emulsify the pieces of your life back to God. Amazingly, even on the cross they gave him vinegar to drink adding another culinary image to this story of salvation.

Give Jesus the chance to make you a new creature, a sauce fit for a king, and He will do it. Only after your life is re-united with God will it have true meaning. God will cause a beauty to come out in your life that will have fragrance and flavor to it. It will be refreshing to all those in your life and those around you. It will be like the finest béarnaise draped over a tender filet or the most delicate hollandaise laced on top of a moist poached egg. Without Him, your life is as a cruet of vinegar on a dusty restaurant table never able to enjoy the pleasure of being married to the oil of heaven. The story of salvation as seen through a hollandaise sauce is amazing.

CHAPTER 5

Hunger for God

As seen through the table of fellowship

"Sharing food with another human being is an intimate act that should not be indulged in lightly.'

- M. F. K. Fisher

"Blessed are those who hunger and thirst for righteousness, for they shall be filled."

- Matthew 5:6

At our house, whenever I cook for guests, the one thought that always comes to mind is; I hope they're hungry! I can't help it – it pops its head up - nudging me into a series of questions... questions that begin the process of analyzing every item I have prepared. It usually starts like this: I wonder if they're hungry. I hope they're hungry. They had better be hungry – I made way too much food. Did I forget anything?

Starting with the first course and moving towards the last course I taste and re-taste everything. It is not that I am insecure of my cooking ability it's just that they are guests in my home, eating at my table, partaking in an intimate, private event, an event where we bare our souls and feelings to each other in that magnificent experience called fellowship.

In this crazy, fast passed, world we live in, have we learned the importance of opening up to one another and baring our hearts – being vulnerable one another? It is more than a meal – it is fellowship with my family. I want them to be blessed... overly blessed.... I want them to be far more satisfied when they depart than when they arrived. I want to exceed their expectations. In a word, "stuffed." I want them to roll out of my house with thoughts that are memorable and will be etched upon their minds forever. I want the taste of our time together to linger and be a point of remembrance for years to come.

The meal is only half of the equation. The other half takes place as we pour out our lives to each other... laughing, telling stories, and listening to all the details about the lives of our guests as we share with each other our triumphs and victories or our concerns, troubles and failures. It is fellowship and it is wonderful!

It never fails, as sure as I am sitting here, the crowd is always hungry. Though I am not sure which hunger is greater, the hunger for food or the hunger for fellowship. I am inclined to believe that real fellowship outweighs the hunger for food. When I stop and think about it, I believe that the hunger for sharing is far greater than the desire to eat. It is almost a case of companionship malnutrition.

Society is missing this, though I truly believe they are hungry for it. Society has a void and its called community and fellowship. We consume but don't communicate. I don't know when this spiritual nutrition deficiency entered into society but my guess is that it crept in, much like that old story of the frog in the pot of boiling water. You see a frog is an interesting little creature. If you were to take a frog and drop him in a pot of boiling water, the moment the frog encounters the water, its adrenalin kicks in and it leaps out of the pot in an effort to stay alive.

On the other hand, if you place the frog in a pot of cold water and turn up the heat slowly, the frog will swim around and around, past the boiling point, until it dies, never making an effort to escape. The frog's body and mind become numb to its environment. The frog becomes complacent and its survival intuitions dull – unable to react to the dangers that surround it. It's like not seeing the forest from the trees – everything is one big blur, and that is what happened to us.

Over the last sixty years, humanity has found itself in the same pot of cold water as that frog. The only difference is that the heat in this situation has been the tolerance to the breakdown of the family, fellowship, and companionship with each other. Prior to the last half of the twentieth century, families, neighbors, towns, cities, and communities were different. The family routinely dined together every night. On weekends it expanded to extended family and friends. Quarterly, there were have family reunions, block parties, and neighborhood festivals. The celebration of the holidays would come along and for thousands of years humanity understood the meaning of community, neighbors, and family relationship.

As I look at the evolution of cuisine over the last fifty years I am amazed at the parallels between how we eat, how we interact as family, and how we interact with God. It appears that this breakdown in Western society started to take place during the beginning of the industrial revolution, when the introduction of the first lunch wagons were born in the 1890s. It would not be long before the advancement in automation and industrial production brought us the first Automat.

The Horn & Hardart Automat opened on Broadway in Times Square in 1912. It was an ornate restaurant with mosaic-tiled floors and marble tabletops. It was the pinnacle of self-service efficiency where the human bridge of cooking and eating was replaced by coin-operated, vending machines, in which pre-cooked foods were displayed in glass windows allowing the customers to see what he or she was getting before buying it. It was automation at its finest, no more waiting in lines at the local cafeteria or talking to employees behind a counter.

All you had to do was stay to yourself, pick your pleasure, and head to a table where you can consume your lunch in the quietness of your own space. These coin-operated machines were progress. They were a tribute to the great industrial age and the evolution of humankind. You longer had to worry about germs in a restaurant; everything was white and shiny with glass and tile.

For the next twenty to thirty years, dining evolved to tidy little restaurants where cooking in front of street patrons through a big glass storefront window, was prevalent as a marketing tool to bring in guests. This gave birth to the modest diner and counter seating where the cooks and servers were right in front of you. Life was good and so were the waffles. A hot cup of coffee, the morning paper, and a piece of pie were all a fellow needed to get the day started…. At least up until 1948 , at the birth of the McDonald brother's "Speedee Service System."

Prior to 1948, the automobile was in full swing. Trolley cars were on their way out and cars were in and in for good. Before this "Speedee Service System" drive-ins were the rage. Lunch and dinner had finely been moved from the kitchen table to the front seat of a car. People still managed to interact with one another and drive-ins soon became the hangout for America's youth.

Instead of roller-bladed tray service by teenage carhops, all one had to do was simply drive up to a window or walk into a counter and order their food. Everything that had to be eaten with a knife, fork, or spoon was taken off the menu and the only sandwiches that were sold were hamburgers. Everything was wrapped in paper or served on plastic.

It wouldn't take long for the effects of fast food to impact every facet of our society. Families getting together for dinner and fellowship have almost disappeared. This cookie-cutter conformity has been felt around the globe. According to Eric Schlosser, in his book Fast Food Nation, states,

> *"An industry that began with a handful of modest hot dog and hamburger stands in southern California has spread to every corner of the nation, selling a broad range of foods wherever paying customers may be found. Fast food is now served at restaurants and drive-throughs, at stadiums, airports, zoos, high schools, elementary schools, and universities, on cruse ships, trains, and airplanes, at K-marts, Wal-Marts, gas stations, and even at hospital cafeterias. In 1970, Americans spent $6 billion on fast food; in 2000, they spent more than $110 billion. Americans now spend more money on fast food than on higher education, personal computers, computer software, or new cars...."*

At the same time we saw the birth of the TV dinner. Frozen metal trays of prepared food resting on TV trays in front of the new revolutionary TV replaced the family meal. The fifties family, sitting in the living room, each with their TV dinner on their TV tray, watching "Leave it to Beaver", was evolving to the new family dining table. Ironically, the act of family fellowship was replaced by watching a make-believe TV family doing on TV what they now do on TV trays.

It was not only those in the fifties that had a hunger for watching shows that portrayed what they were missing. Consider the following (I know I am aging myself):

- The Brady Bunch
- Gilligan's Island
- Gidget
- Lost in Space
- Fat Albert
- Fantasy Island
- The Love Boat

And who can forget the wonderful Mr. Rogers, when he sang:

> "It's a beautiful day in the neighborhood, a beautiful day for a neighbor – Would you be mine? Could you be mine? Won't you be my neighbor?"

Looking back at the subtle erosion of family values that were once united around the dinner table, I have to stop and ask what happened. I know there is a hunger; you see it everywhere you go. Look at the millions that turn in weekly to the Food-Network, or the millions that recapture fellowship with the weekend barbeque, they are hungry for this community of fellowship, they desire to get back some of what was lost, but its on a surface level. No one really knows this hunger exists. They scratch at it but they really know its' a hunger. Of course, Americans, as a whole, really don't understand hunger. Unless they grew up in the great depression, hunger is foreign to them.

Even our relationship in church and with God has been tainted by this fast-food-no-time-for-fellowship mentality. The commercialization of the local church has taken on new heights and theme park attributes. Flash and well-regimented 45-minute sermons neatly tucked into our busy schedules are the mood of the day. We even have churches that offer drive-in services so you do not need to get out of your car. What is wrong with this picture?

When the Father is preparing a meal at the table of fellowship – He asks the same questions I asked before my guests arrive. I wonder if they are hungry. I wonder if they will be on time – it is getting short and I don't want anyone to miss out on what I have prepared for them. I made way too much food and am overflowing with blessing for them.

Nevertheless, all too often, because of our lack of hunger for him, we nibble at the crumbs that have fallen off His lap instead of feasting at the meal he has set before us. I pray that in these last days we will learn what true hunger is, what it means to hunger and thirst after God. We must respond to the intervention that he has sent to us – we must be diligent and R.S.V.P. – ASAP.

Answer this question: Has fast food impacted your taste buds and your desire for quality? Has fast church with little fellowship degraded your taste buds for the deeper things of God? You see, like the ready-to-eat fast food burger, which scientifically has been produced in a food-lab with just the right amount of fat, moisture, texture, salt and so on, so that it will have mass appeal and satisfy the majority of eaters, so we have programmed our church agenda. Are we satisfied with 1.5-hour commitment to God one day a week? Are we OK with struggling through a sermon with no fire or passion? Where is the hunger? Where is our relationship with God? What level of Holy cuisine are we striving for? Are we looking for His finest meal or are we settling for a quick drive-through relationship?

Not only are we not hungry for more of Him, but also programmed to settle for the neat and orderly fast-food church experience. There is richness and depth in the meal Jesus desires to prepare for us. We need to learn the meaning of hunger. We need to learn to activate our senses and seek more than crumbs from the table.

There is a meal being prepared for the church. A supper from heaven is cooking and God is sending out an invitation. He is searching the highways and byways looking for those who are hungry enough to come to the banquet and fellowship with Him, for God has said, taste and see that the Lord is good!

I want you to do something. I want you to stop right now, and do two things: First, I want you to ask yourself – "How hungry am I?" When you do this, don't look at your hunger as a quick bite. Don't even look at it as a late night snack. Instead, picture in your mind those little starving children in depressed areas of the world, whose bellies are swollen from malnutrition. Place that picture over your spiritual mind and ask the same question – "Am I hungry for Christ, as that child is for food?" If you're not, you're not truly hungry. Secondly, ask yourself this question – Have my taste buds been numbed to accept the crumbs off the Master's table, or a spiritual "Big Mac," instead of the fullness that God wants to give you? Many times, we accept the good things of God, over and above, His BEST things. We would rather sit in the car and eat a burger than feast on that big juicy porterhouse just off the barbeque of His presence. Pray that God will revitalize your taste buds and your hunger for His very best. That is His desire. He is prepping the wedding feast of the Lamb and you are invited! Remember - Blessed are those who hunger and thirst after righteousness, for they shall be filled.

Chapter 6

Spiritual Growth

As seen through a loaf of bread

"Brown bread and the gospel is good fare."

- Puritans

"Without bread all is misery."

- William Cobbet

"Go pound some dough in your kitchen after work, and find out what tasty therapy it can be."

- Wolfgang Puck

I was fifteen the first time I witnessed the art of true bread making. I mean production bread making, the kind of bread that comes out of the oven like a company of marines de-boarding a landing craft. The loaves were massive three pounders of old-fashioned crusty deli rye. The oven was an old black rotary deck oven that had four, 12-foot shelves, mounted on vertical axis and rotated merry-go-round style. It was 13 feet wide, 10 feet tall and 10 feet deep. When full, the oven held 48 - 18" x 26" Bun pans with 4 loaves per pan or 192 loaves of bread.

I worked at Kaplan's Jewish deli as a kid, located at the South Coast Plaza Mall, in Costa Mesa, California. I just turned fifteen and was excited at the opportunity to work there. It was the busiest restaurant in town, you couldn't beat the sandwiches – mile-high hot corned beef on freshly baked rye with good mustard, and melted Swiss cheese. It was a taste of heaven. All the sandwiches were made fresh to order.

I would get an order for say, a number 14 (a double-decker of hot pastrami, hot corned beef, Swiss cheese, thousand island, and coleslaw, mounded high between three slices of hot rye bread). The first step was to reach down into this massive, 4' x 3', stainless steal steam bin, and with my 14" meat fork, pull out two hot briskets, one pastrami and the other corned beef. I had three slicers positioned to my right, one for pastrami, one for corned beef, and the third for loaves of hot fresh baked rye bread. I placed the brisket on my cutting board, and with my slicing knife I removed the fat that that lies between the two plates of the brisket. I placed the brisket on the slicer and sliced off about 3 ounces of each meat, as thin as possible, rolling the meat with my hands into a lose ball, and onto the freshly sliced bread with the other ingredients. With two, three-inch frill picks stuck into each half of the sandwich, I would cut it in half, plate it up, and off it went to the guest.

It was a wonderful thing to serve a quality sandwich. I learned much during my time working there. I was introduced to many different types of deli food from kishka to matzo balls everything was delightful.

I started out as a line cook working the morning shift. I loved this shift, and I loved to cook breakfast and lunch. One of the real treats was working with the bakers. They arrived early – very early, around three in the morning. That was way too early for me, but I had no problem getting there at five. That gave me about a half hour to watch the bakers do their magic. I was curious about those old bakers. They kept to themselves, a private club if you will. All the cooks hung-out but the bakers were a group unto themselves. I think they let me watch because I was the first one that ever really cared to. The time at the deli was good for me. It gave me the foundation for a love of bread and the beauty of its simplicity and contribution to food and life that has been with me ever since.

You can say, I am a bread lover – or a lover of *fine* breads. I am not talking about bleached white air-infused loaves that you buy to anchor the ends of a baloney or peanut butter sandwich. I'm talking about real bread. Real bread has aroma, texture, taste, and warmth. It awakens all five senses. I'm talking about bread that has been prepared with love, kindness, and above all, respect. I'm talking about the type of bread that crackles as the cool night air encounters the crust while it's cooling. Home baked bread is the bread for me. It is so full of life that the dough must have touched the heart of the baker before it came out of the oven. I think Huckleberry Finn said it best when he was baited by it's sweet aroma.

> *"A big double loaf came along, and I most got it with a long stick, but my foot slipped and she floated out further.... But by and by along comes another one, and this time I won. I took out the plug and shook out this little dab of quicksilver, and set my teeth in. It was 'baker's bread' – what the quality eat; none of your low-down corn-pone."*

There are three basic types of bread:

- Yeast
- Quick
- Unleavened

Yeast breads are leavened with yeast. Within the yeast bread family you find two basic types – dough and batter. Gluten is the key to good dough bread. In order for dough to be effective, it must be kneaded to form gluten. When you add water to wheat flour and stir, two proteins, glutenin and gliadin, grab each other as and combine with the water. As you continue to work or knead the flour, more and more of these proteins connect and cross-connect to form sheets of gluten. These incredible elastic sheets trap and hold air and gases made by the yeast causing the bread to rise and, as in the case of flat bread, give it elasticity.

Wheat flour is at the heart of this gluteniness process. No other flour has enough of these two proteins to make dough react this way. Of all the grains, corn, oats, rye, rice, or barley, the wheat kernel is the winner in giving dough the ability to trap air and gases, giving us a virtual spectrum of varieties to taste. Wheat kernels contain the bran, the germ, and the endosperm, which are the starch and the protein.

When wheat milling takes place, the kernels are cleaned and soaked in water to remove the germ and the bran. The kernels are crushed and the bran and germ are separated. As a miller grinds and sifts the endosperm it gets broken up into what is called streams. These streams of wheat are what make the different types of flour. Streams that are high in protein are what are used in bread flour. High-protein flour will form great sheets of gluten and are perfect for dough that needs the elasticity for holding yeast. Cake flour, on the other hand, is low-protein flour and gives the product lightness. While at the same time, whole-wheat flour, which is high in protein, but also includes the germ and the bran, will make the bread heavy and unable to form gluten in the same way as white bread flour.

The right flour is all there is standing between a good loaf of bread and a pour one. A loaf of bread made with high protein bread flour will rise and bake into a nice airy loaf with a nice golden crust color. Yet, if you try to make that same loaf with all-purpose flour, you will end up with a heavy dense, brick – good only for bookends or paperweights.

Not only does the type of flour used effect how gluten is formed, each flour type absorbs water differently, that is why, when you see in recipes "approximations" such as – "use 2-3 cups of all purpose flour" – what they are telling you is to use as much as is needed, based on how it absorbs the water. All-purpose flour is different all over the country, even in a generic name brand, you cannot be sure it is the same kind of flour the recipe calls for. The following illustrates my point.

Flour Protein Percent

- Southern all-purpose: 7.5 to 9.5%
- National Brand all-purpose: 9.5 to 12%
- Northern all-purpose: 11 to 12%
- Cake flour: 7.5 to 8.5%
- National Brand self-rising flour: 9 to 10%

One way you can be sure of what type of flour you have is to see how it absorbs water. Flour that absorbs a lot of water is high in protein and good for yeast breads, the less absorption – the less protein.

When I think of the dynamics of bread, I am reminded of a vision the Lord gave me several years ago that touched my heart in a time of deep distress. This background on bread I gave you is essential in understanding this vision.

I Knead You!

Have you ever had one of those times in your life where it seemed that God was nowhere around? Or, that your prayers felt as if they were bouncing off the heavens like an iron ceiling? I have found that life often revolves around seasons of dichotomy where you experience the heights of the mountaintops, but much in the valleys between. The walk in the valley may be a lonely time but it is an important time. It is the season that God uses to build your faith and expand His presence in your life.

I was in one of those seasons. I had been truly seeking God's face, desiring Him to change me and draw me closer to Him. I was struggling with my past and the luggage I carried in to my Christian life. I was having a hard time dealing with my past and struggled with God's mercy and grace.

I was attending a home fellowship group. I had confessed to the group that I felt very dry and alone in my walk with God. I asked if they could pray with me. During prayer, the Lord gave me the following vision:

> *I saw a river flowing through the center of a desert wasteland. Jesus was standing next to the river with a bundle of wheat in*

His hand. Next to Him was a large flat rock about the size and shape of an end table.

The Lord took the wheat in His hand and began to beat it against the rock and let the kernels of wheat fall onto the rock.

Then He held up the wheat, let the wind blow away the chaff, and shook it over the rock to let the remaining grains fall. Jesus took the wheat and began to grind it with the palm of his hand into the rock.

As he ground the wheat, He dipped His hand into the river, scoping out a handful of water, and sprinkled it over the ground wheat, grinding and working it with His hands, until he had formed a dough ball.

*All of a sudden, Jesus stopped what He was doing and looked into my eyes and said – "I **knead you!**"*

I was blown away by the parable of the vision - I began to cry. I knew immediately what He was saying to me. The desert place in the vision was where I was at in my walk. Jesus knew exactly where I was and what I was feeling. The river was that river of God that always flows, no matter where we are. He is a river of living water. He meets us where we are at, to quench the thirst of a dry and weary soul.

The wheat symbolized my life and the shaking of the wheat was the Holy Spirit's sanctifying work in my life, removing the things that are unpleasant in God's sight, and preparing kernels of wheat that have a substance and a depth to them. The process of grinding the wheat and mixing the flour and the water to make dough is the process of building character and infusing my life with faith that will endure during the tough times.

The same process of working dough to build a web of gluten – the Holy Spirit works in our lives to build a spiritual glutinous web that will trap the breath of His Spirit and cause us to rise to the occasion of our calling in him. The whole message to me was a double-sided message. Jesus was saying – I knead you because I need you.

In other words, the wilderness you are experiencing and the dryness you may feel at times is a process that is vital to your spiritual growth so that you are enabled to receive what God desires to do in your life. The road to growth is a road filled with moments that stretch your faith and bring elasticity into your life, causing you to stretch way beyond your own natural abilities.

In a way, God works in our lives as a master baker preparing dough that is fit for the oven. The bread that God wants to make out of your lives is bread that has aroma, texture, taste, and warmth; it awakens the souls of those around you - it is the extension of the bread of life – which Christ desires to feed to the world.

When you are experiencing those times of dryness or feeling alone, and frustrated, in your walk with the Lord maybe you are in a season of preparation. Maybe it's a time at the baker's table where Jesus is working through the details of your life to build your faith and give you a new strength and stability that you would not experience lest you go through the kneading process.

Remember Jesus truly loves you and He kneads you more than you can imagine. Let Jesus knead the dough of your soul so that you will be all you were created to be. Enjoy the culinary greatness of good homemade bread. Do this, the next time you eat or bake a loaf of bread… recognize the symbolism, and ask God to knead your life and infuse it with the wonders of the Master Baker.

CHAPTER 7

The Bread of Life

As seen through fresh Matzoth

> *"Therefore let us keep the feast, not with old leaven, nor with the leaven of malice and wickedness, but with the unleavened bread of sincerity and truth"*
>
> - 1 Corinthians 5:8

Have you ever eaten fresh matzoth? Not the stuff that comes in a box like you find at your local grocer, but the kind that is eaten minutes out of the oven. Matzoth is one of the oldest bread in history. Matzoth is unleavened flatbread that our Jewish brothers and sisters eat during the celebration of Passover and was no doubt the bread that Jesus broke during the Last Supper on that Passover weekend some 2,000 years ago.

The symbolism of Matzoth is far reaching throughout scripture and the Passover is mentioned in Exodus

23:14-17, Numbers 28, Leviticus 23, Ezra 6, and in 1 Corinthians 5:7 where Paul calls Christ our Passover. Leaven was considered a symbol of sin thus the Passover feast was also called the feast of Unleavened Bread. In looking at the parabolic nature of unleavened bread, Paul, in 1 Corinthians 5:8, challenges Christians to put away the "*old leaven*" of malice and wickedness and replace it with "*the unleavened bread of sincerity and truth.*"

Therefore, if one is of the Jewish faith or the Christian faith – Matzoth is a symbol we all should contemplate. To both, the Christian and the Jew, the Passover has powerful significance. To the Christian, it is the cornerstone of salvation, the sacrificial act of Christ on the cross. To the Jew, it is an anchor within their faith, a release from bondage and a bridge to the Promised Land. But more it is a message of the true manna that came down from heaven and the ongoing promise of the Messiah's coming and His redemptive plan.

Jews have suffered more than any other group of people in history. The second book of the Torah, or Pentateuch, is the book of the Bible that outlines the plight of Jewish people out of Egypt and into the Promised Land. The journey was long and treacherous. It is one that shows us the heights of the faithful and the depths of the faithless. It is dramatic and provides an essential background for all that follows in the rest of the book. It centers on the call of Moses, one of the most pivotal men of all history. It is about the family of Jacob, who had migrated to Egypt in the Book of Genesis, and now emerges as a nation. The plight of Israel under the taskmasters of Egypt leads to the famed Passover and deliverance of God's chosen people. It continues to this day as one of their principal observances in the Jewish custom.

In fact, the instruction to the nation was to make this month (Nisan/April) "the beginning of months." Thus, Israel has two calendars; one, their civil calendar, which begins in the fall (Tishri, about September/October on our calendar); the other, their religious calendar, which begins in the spring (Nisan, about April/May on our calendar.)

Interestingly, John the Baptist's first public introduction of Jesus declared, *"Behold the Lamb of God that takes away the sin of the world,"* points to the Passover Lamb. The Lamb of God has redeemed us from our sins and has washed us from all iniquity. It is this very Lamb of God that is at work in our lives every single day of our lives. Sometimes it is easy to forget how committed Jesus is to us. The Passover was the feast that God initiated, to implant in the heart of the Jewish people His faithfulness. He didn't want them to forget what He had done delivering them from the powers of the Pharaoh and bringing them into a new salvation. For Christians this bread a very powerful tool used in remembering all that Christ has done for us.

When I look at Matzoth, I see bread that is rich with spiritual lessons for family, friends, and loved ones. It is one of those breads that you can make as a group and use the opportunity to share the love of Christ with those you are eating. Remember, "*Man shall not live by bread alone*" as Jesus, declared, "*I am the bread of Life...*" which is the only source for true spiritual nourishment.

Matzoth is bread made from flour and water with no salt, no oil, and no yeast. In Judaism, Matzoth is eaten during Passover to commemorate the speed at which Moses led the Jewish people out of Egypt.

The story of the first Passover

"Now these are the names of the children of Israel who came to Egypt; each man and his household came with Jacob: Reuben, Simeon, Levi, and Judah; Issachar, Zebulun, and Benjamin; Dan, Naphtali, Gad, and Asher. All those who were descendants of Jacob were seventy persons (for Joseph was in Egypt already). And Joseph died, all his brothers, and all that generation. But the children of Israel were fruitful and increased abundantly, multiplied and grew exceedingly mighty; and the land was filled with them.

Now there arose a new king over Egypt, who did not know Joseph. And he said to his people, "Look, the people of the children of Israel are more and mightier than we; come, let us deal shrewdly with them, lest they multiply, and it happen, in the event of war, that they also join our enemies and fight against us, and so go up out of the land." Therefore they set taskmasters over them to afflict them with their burdens. And they built for Pharaoh supply cities, Pithom and Raamses. But the more they afflicted them, the more they multiplied and grew. And they were in dread of the children of Israel...."

- Exodus 12:1-12

Warm Matzoth is good, but what is even more exciting is the fellowship you can have while preparing this bread. It is the perfect accompaniment that entire family can make together and is perfect for sharing the message of Jesus Christ with your kids or with company. Use the kitchen as a platform to share your faith with others or to teach your children about the truth of scripture. You could be baking bread, cookies, matzoth, salad, or homemade mayonnaise... it doesn't matter.

The kitchen can be the best place in the family to teach, share, and have fellowship. Remember – all around you the gospel cries out to be told – stop – look around – and let the Holy Spirit show you Jesus in the everyday things that surround you. Invite the Holy Spirit in the kitchen and transform everyday activities into life giving moments of fellowship. After all, that is what Jesus did.

Matzoth Recipe

2 cups white flour

1/2 tablespoon freshly ground black pepper

2 eggs

3 tablespoons honey

1/2 tablespoon extra-virgin olive oil

4 tablespoons water

Procedures

Preheat oven to 400 degrees. In a large bowl, combine the flour and pepper. Stir together the eggs, honey, oil and water; pour over the dry ingredients and mix just until combined.

Turn the dough out onto a countertop and knead until it forms a cohesive ball.

Divide the dough into 6 portions. One by one, roll them out into 8-inch rounds; prick all over with a fork, then place onto a very lightly greased baking sheet.

Bake for 10 minutes, until crisp and golden. Let cool completely on a rack.

Repeat with remaining dough, to make 6 each.

CHAPTER 8

O' Bethlehem

As seen through the neighborhood restaurant

"Behold, the days are coming, says the Lord God, 'That I will send a famine on the land, Not a famine of bread, Nor a thirst for water, But of hearing the words of the Lord. They shall wander from sea to sea, And from north to east; They shall run to and fro, seeking the word of the Lord, But shall not find it.'"

- Amos 5:11-12

"The average church has so much machinery and so little oil of the Holy Spirit that it squeaks like a threshing machine when you start it up in the fall after it has been out in the field all year."

- Billy Sunday (1862–1935)

The problem with restaurants today is the same problem we see in many of our churches. Let me explane. The French were the first to coin the word "Restaurant." In the Dictionnaire de Trevoux, in 1771, defined the word restaurateur, as:

> *"Someone who has the art of preparing true broths, known as 'restaurants', and the right to sell all kinds of custards, dishes of rice, vermicelli and macaroni, egg dishes, boiled capons, preserved and stewed fruit and other delicious and healthy-giving foods."*

It wasn't until 1786 that the word restaurant was used to describe a eating-house. Paris was booming with social eateries. The simplicity of the early eating-houses was nothing like the restaurants of nineteenth century. They were local hangouts – places that served comfort food – honest, homemade, and at a value that was friendly to the working class of the day. What had started out as a simple house-of-bread had suddenly become more complex and compared to that first little café in 1550 Constantinople, unrecognizable. Whether you dined in a café, bistro, brasserie, or an elegant restaurant, dining was the social fashion of nineteenth century Europe.

Today, eating-houses are big business – and we are inundated with them. They line up like merchant-booths in an ancient marketplace, waiting for the crowds to sample their wares – we have them on every street corner, and on every inch of space in-between, cookie-cutter concepts that unfold, pop-up, and spread out across the landscape like settler's tents across the prairie planes. No longer is the sole-proprietor standing at the door to great you. No longer do you walk into a neighborhood café and have intimacy with the owner and your fellow patrons.

The days of the independent owner, who had only one goal in mind, to fill the place with well nourished, extremely stuffed, and happy consumers, is over. It doesn't matter what you call it, a Café, Bistro, Brasserie, Tavern, Diner, Coffee Shop, or Restaurant, if there's one on every street corner you can be guaranteed the menu as well as the experience is carved out of the boardroom and not from the heart of a chef proprietor.

The days of the community restaurant beating with the heart-felt passion of an independent neighborhood owner is gone in most communities. The independent owner saw their restaurant as a place with a purpose, that people would come in; they'd eat, and be satisfied beyond their expectations. Their experience is so fulfilling, so wonderful, that they leave feeling full and content and they want to come back again. Not only do they come back – they become a marketing-champagne unto themselves. They tell their friends, their neighbors, anyone who will listen, what a grand experience they had in your restaurant.

The sad reality is that many independent restaurants today struggle to survive and are going up neck and neck with the big boys. They loose their footing and barley get by. Month after month they feel trapped in a slow death that doesn't seem to end. They can't compete with the glitz and the glitter of the well-staged cookie-cutter concept of their corporate counterpart. The corporate giants on the other hand have it down pat (at least most of the time).

They have the educated experience, corporate marketing, project planning, a solid infrastructure of controls and training, a pulse on the consumer, and the corporate cash flow to back up their enterprise. They have done their homework and they know the demographics of the area – where to put their hot branded concept. The problem with corporate institutional giants is not their expertise and business acumen. The problem is a lack of passion. It is hard to deliver passion downstream. Some corporations do it well (Apple, Starbucks, Etc.) But on the most part, passion is birthed closed to the door of the concept creator.

Without passion, even though you have all the ingredients of success, you will soon become a whitewashed tomb of a restaurant. You will be a colorful balloon – bright and shiny on the outside – but inside – full of hot air - serving up dribble to a consumer that has lost their ability to taste real food. They have bought into the picture on the billboard with its thick and juicy representation of a dish that in reality is not even close to the picture. Thank heaven for glitz and glitter. If you spin it right, strong theme, lots of energy and glitzy decorative elements to distract them from the product – maybe the folks won't notice… and the sad thing is – most do not.

Yesterday my wife and I were sitting around trying to decide what to eat for dinner. When suddenly, like a moment of marital oneness, we looked at each other and said, "Breakfast." That was it, nothing like steak and eggs with a side of hot flapjacks to wind out the evening. We hopped on my motorcycle and shoot over to a nearby chain coffee shop that recently opened. The building and design package of the facility was nice. They had all the extra consumer hooks one would anticipate these days, retail merchandising at the entrance, walk-up to-go counter for easy pick-up, counter seating with contemporary table-lamps - positioned appropriately, and a warm comfortable interior broken up with a modest ratio of booths and tables. Decorative pony walls and partitions infused with a few plants breaking up the space to create the right environment without causing you to feel you were eating in a banquet hall.

So far so good, I thought to myself, as I reached for the menu to scan the offerings. The menu was, from a corporate standpoint, perfectly engineered. All the items were well placed, descriptors were well written, layout was crisp, and for a café, the offerings sounded appealing. My choice was easy... steak and eggs to feed my craving, and flapjacks – there's nothing like a pancake supper with a good steak and a side of eggs to fill that void.

Well, so much for fantasy, my food arrived and it was awful... I mean BAD, and I haven't said that in a long time. Sitting on my plate was the most puny, overcooked, soggy (figure that one out), piece of what they referred to as a steak. Next to that boil-in-the-bag piece of meat was a small pile of little pail, un-seasoned, cubed potatoes, called home fries, and two pail looking eggs, at least they were over-easy. Now, as I get older I have grown to focus more on the company I keep than the meal, but this time I couldn't. I felt like Howard Beale (played by Peter Finch), the acclaimed news anchorman for UBS TV in that 1976 movie "Network." I wanted to stand up and look at the rest of the patrons in the restaurant and say,

> "Look at your food – look at it will you and ...get up now. I want all of you to get up out of your chairs. I want you to get up right now and go to the window, open it, and stick your head out and yell, I'm as mad as hell, and I'm not going to take this anymore!!"

Ah, but alas, I contained myself. With a loss of appetite, I returned my food and sat there with a warm cup of coffee. I continued a nice dialog with my wife while waiting patently to depart.

You see, this place with all the components to make a modern day restaurant a success lacked one serious ingredient. They could not deliver what they had promised – good food. It takes passion to make good food. Someone in the kitchen has to be on his or her knees before a hot stove and find out how and what to cook.

Passion is the key that that separates real food from a cheap imitation. Passion is the door, the driving force, which brings all the right elements together. Passion will pull you to the consumer's table to check the pulse of their experience. Passion will drive you into the kitchen causing you work endlessly on a dish, over, and over again, until it is just right, its taste, texture, aroma, the layers of flavor, and its presentation, all of it. You will tear it apart and build it back up again – as many times as needed until it's right.

Passion is contagious. Passion is contagious with the staff and the patron. People are drawn to your passion. People want to be around people that believe... people that are truly excited about what they do. They want to brush up against you and get close to you. They want to catch a glimpse of something. They want to glean a new understanding the depth of what you're doing. They want an imparting of something. They want your mantel – they want a double dose of the fire that is burning inside of you. They want to draw from the wellspring of your experience. They desire to taste of something grand. They want their cups to overflow.

Now listen... this is very important. I am not talking about restaurants, corporations, or the consumer. **I am talking about the Church** – that great mystery that Paul spoke of – the bride of Christ. I am talking about the great commission. I am talking about the Master Chef – Jesus Christ, and His desire to set a table in the community where you live and serve up a meal that is fit for Priests and Kings. I am talking about Passion and the Pulpit. I am talking about the ingredients needed to reach a dying world. I am talking about the difference between a lukewarm church or dead church and one that is alive on the in side with the presence and heartbeat of Jesus Christ.

The restaurant, in a real way, is parallel to our church buildings today. We build them virtually on every street corner. We offer up verbal menus from the Word of God for all to come and feast upon, both sinner and saint. We desire to restore man back into fellowship with their loving Father and introduce them to the bread of life. Even the word "Restaurant" has its root meaning "to restore; a food that restores," and aren't we, as the body of Christ, been given the great commission to restore mankind back into fellowship with their creator, to feed them real bread, living bread, the bread of life.

Often, we the church, have bought in to this corporate model. Instead of spending time on our knees before the hot stove of God's presence, we are in search for the right hook, a good program, and a new way to increase the tithe and raise the membership. Our real model is closer to Jesus in the garden of Gethsemane, than the hanging gardens of Babylon. We don't need spin we need to be spent, like change in the pocket of an Almighty God. We need to be sold out to Him. We need to seek Him until we sweat, as it were, great drops of blood. Only then will we have a message that is birthed in travail. Only then will we communicate the "Passion of Christ."

We get caught up in our various programs and events, how well we say the same old message, while forgetting what the fundamental mission that brought us here to begin with. At times such as this, we have to go back to our first love and receive from Him the passion and simplicity that we knew when we first believed – where the mission was fresh and simplistic – the goals were souls and not much more.

That is not always a simple task. People have a tendency to get comfortable no matter where they are or in what state they are. They settle into complacency and loose the desire for a deep love relationship. It becomes a forked-road marriage where each partner is headed in opposite directions. Neither a marriage nor the church will be able to survive in a state as that. We, the bride of Christ, must be in submissive obedience to His master plan. Our churches need more of Him and less of us.

It's just like that cookie-cutter restaurant my wife and I were eating at, it looked good, had all the spin, but in the end there was nothing solid to eat. It had become a "house-of-stale-bread" or a "house-of-bread" serving no bread at all, just old dried crumbs ground into the carpets from patrons long forgotten. When a restaurant runs out of its ability to serve food – people stop coming. The sad thing is that these people are hungry – they are thirsty – they are looking for someone somewhere to open their doors and invite them to come in and feast at the table of abundance.

The church, tragically, and often, has end up in the same condition. A house-of-bread where the only mandate is to reminisce about the bread of the past – speculating how good it must have tasted. Yet, there are no ovens to bake what the people want or need. It becomes a history lesson about bread. People come in hungry for the bread of life. They want to sink their teeth into savory hot loaves of freshly baked bread. They hunger and desire manna from heaven but all they get is a menu they can never order off of.

Oh, there's talk about how wonderful the bread once was – they even sing about bread – but serve it fresh and hot – no way. All of this brings about a spiritual famine in the land. People go about their day hungry and thirsty for a living vibrant relationship with the bread of life – but are left unfilled and hopeless. The sad thing is that Jesus is more, now than ever before, ready to send fresh hot loves of His presence into their midst – if they would only seek His face and give Him back His church.

So what happens to the communities where we live, our neighborhoods, and our cities? What happens to our children? What happens to all the starving people around us desiring to sink their teeth into spiritual food that has substance and life giving power? They go hungry and the famine becomes more rigorous. Our churches become fast food outlets – scattered about on every street corner – but nothing of substance is really served there.

What do people do when their spiritual hunger becomes spiritual malnutrition? They flock to anything or anyone that offers something resembling a loaf of bread. They window-shop on the streets of our cities and taste the offerings of the new age movement, Eastern mysticism, or the occult, in search for hot bread. They seek out astrologers and tarot card readers hoping to find living water to quench their dying souls.

People are a lot smarter than we think. If one of our churches lit the ovens of the Holy Spirit and started cooking hot loaves from heaven – word would travel! It would get around! People would do anything to get real bread – hot freshly baked bread – especially in times of great famine.

Consider the story of Ruth, found in the book of Ruth in the Old Testament.

> *"Now it came to pass, in the days when the judges ruled, that there was a famine in the land. And a certain man of Bethlehem, Judah, went to dwell in the country of Moab, he and his wife and his two sons...*
>
> *... Then she arose with her daughters-in-law that she might return from the country of Moab, for she had heard in the country of Moab that the Lord had visited His people by giving them bread."*

- Ruth 1:1, 6

Naomi and her family left home and moved to Moab because there was a famine in Bethlehem. Bethlehem was the city of David. Bethlehem was the birthplace of the

Messiah. Bethlehem was the birthplace of the bread of life. Bethlehem was the last place on earth you would think of as a place of famine. Even the literal translation of Bethlehem in the Hebrew means "*the House of Bread*." It should not have been a place of famine, but famine came, and Naomi left because they were hungry. They left because the **House of Bread had no bread at all.**

Why do people leave or never come into our churches? The answer is, because there is no bread! Bread is the substance for life. The Jews knew the power of bread. They used its symbolism during the Passover (feast of unleavened bread). The showbread was an integral part of the tabernacle and proof of the presence of God in the temple. In the book of Numbers, chapter four, it was called the bread of the Presence. The showbread literally means – *show-up bread* – the evidence that God has shown up in this place.

Naomi and her family are symbolic of the people that never enter or leave many of our churches today. They left Bethlehem and went to Moab trying to find bread. Oh what lengths people will go through in search of some hot bread in times of famine.

We see it all around us – people flock to nightclubs, casinos, and bars, in search for bread that will fill the void in their souls. They become slaves to sin, drugs, mental or physical abuse, and they except it – believing it is their cup in life. Why do they believe this? The answer is simple, we have let them down, and we have failed them and not offered them the reality of the living truth and the power of a gospel that will change their lives forever. We have become a franchise of the fast food gospel.

The good news is we do not have to except this state of spiritual melancholy. Jesus is more than ready to rain upon us manna from heaven. He wants His church back and is more than ready to hang a sign outside the "House of Bread" stating – Welcome... Under New Management! The turnaround is simple,

> *"If My people who are called by My name will humble themselves, and pray and seek My face, and turn from their wicked ways, then I will hear from heaven, and will forgive their sin and heal their land."*

- 2 Chronicles 7:14

There is no other way. God wants to bake loaves of hot bread and serve them up with the olive oil of His presence.

The next time you drive down the restaurant district of your neighborhood pay attention to all the types of restaurants you find there. Look at the ones that have a two-hour wait, in contrast to the restaurants whose parking lots are empty. Count the number of fast food outlets and cookie-cutter chains, and see how many cars are lined up in the drive-thru. Look at the churches in your neighborhood and use they same kind of guidelines as you try to find the one with a two-hour wait – to get in.

They question is, why are they there? Is it because the food is great or because they have become numb and their taste buds have been dulled to accept whatever is put before them? Are they there because, really, that's the best we have to offer and nothing better? I tell you, if a Great restaurant opened its doors and served hot-out-of-the-oven bread, you would have to fight them off with a stick.

I challenge you – if people are willing to stand in line for two-hours to have a burger – how long will they stand in front of a church that is overflowing with the presence and power of the Holy Spirit. The bread-of-life will draw them. The water will keep them. No coupon or two-for-ones will bring them in. No early bird specials will cause them to beat down your doors. However, bread, life-giving bread, just out of the oven bread, served hot and fresh for this generation – will.

Humanity has a bread-shaped hole in its heart and the only thing that will fill it is Jesus. Let's get back to the culinary basics and bring forth hot bread to the nations. I look forward to the day when the lines outside our churches go on for blocks. I can't wait for the sweet aroma of the freshly baked bread of His presence to float through our streets filling the air like incense, drawing all those who are tired and needy. I look forward to the time when restaurant owners have to close down their restaurants because the ovens are turned up at the church down the street – fresh bread is being served and the entire town is eating it up. Let's get on with the task at hand. Light the fire – kindle the stove –

turn up the heat – let Jesus show up and bring to the world the bread of His presence.

"But you, Bethlehem Ephrathah,

Though you are little among the thousands of Judah,

Yet out of you shall come forth to Me

The One to be Ruler in Israel,

Whose goings forth are from of old,

From everlasting."

- Micah 5:2

CHAPTER 9

Sanctification

As seen through the making of a consommé

"I would often ask the butcher, in those days, for a few bones 'for my dog.' Then I would make the most exquisite soup of those bones.... It was several years before my butcher realized that I didn't have a dog."

- Edward Giobbi

"To make a good soup, the pot must only simmer or 'smile.'"

- French Proverb

"Yes, every pot in Jerusalem and Judah shall be holiness to the Lord of hosts. Everyone who sacrifices shall come and take them and cook in them. In that day

> *there shall no longer be a Canaanite in the house of the Lord of hosts."*
>
> - Zechariah 14:21

There I was back in California, right where I started. Only this time I was newly married and a new Christian. I had met my wife while she was on summer break from the university. Jan and her girlfriends had decided to load up the VW and head west.

I bumped into Jan at a waterfront bar, which anchored the pier, in Huntington Beach. I literally bumped into her, spilling my drink all over her new blouse. After walking her home, promising I would get her blouse cleaned and pleading with her to let me see her again, I managed to get her phone number. I spent the next several days trying to get her to go out with me. She lived in an apartment a couple of blocks from my house with her girlfriends. My tenacity won the day and Jan accepted my invitation.

I decided to buy a bottle of Blue Nun and cook up a homemade pizza. It was a big success everyone enjoyed the pizza and the Blue Nun. Later that night we left her roommates and went for a swim in the pool outside her apartment. That was my chance – I will turn on the charm and show her what a great person I was. I started in with my half-baked impressions including the voices of John Wayne, Mr. Roarke from Fantasy Island, and Woody Woodpecker, but the one that sealed my fate forever was the Munchkin song from the Wizard of Oz. We laughed all night till the next morning. Jan and I had hit it off. We spent the entire summer together riding my motorcycle from Palm Springs to Laguna Beach. It was the best summer of our lives. The day finally arrived for Jan and her roommates to head back to school.

I was heart torn that she was leaving. I knew in my heart that Jan was the one for me. I helped them load up their car. We kissed and cried – promising each other that we would call and keep in touch. I couldn't handle her being gone. I was consumed with thoughts of Jan at every waking hour. I decided to go out on a limb. I saved my money, bought a plane ticket to Michigan, and headed east to the land of the Blue and Gold. Jan was going to Western Michigan University at Kalamazoo. She lived in the dorms and had no idea I was headed in her direction.

When I arrived, I asked around for her dorm location. After several wrong attempts, I finally found it and knocked on the door. Jan answered it and the tears began to roll down her face. We hugged, kissed, and talked for several hours. She let me stay the night on the floor, and that morning I asked her to marry me. Jan said yes.

The day came for me to meet her parents. We drove a blue and white 1966 Volkswagen Bus with Hawaiian drapes, a wooden bumper, and a rat-tail glass-pack that stuck out the rear end. We met Jan's dad at a restaurant. After about, what seemed like eternity, I got up the courage to ask Jan's dad for her hand in marriage. We were both a bit frightened but by the end of dinner my soon to be father-in-law agreed to let us marry and begin our life long adventure!

The next day I went out and landed a job at this little French restaurant – Jacques Petit Jardin – right down the street from the Macus Red Fox, the restaurant where Jimmy Hoffa took his last ride. It was a great restaurant owned by Master Chef Stur Olf Andersson, who also was on the 1976/1980 US Culinary Olympic team, and won several gold medals at the International Culinary Olympics in Germany. Stur was my mentor, my father chef, so to speak. I absorbed much from Stur but the greatest gift he had given me was passion. It wasn't soon after Jan and I got married. Chef Andersson catered our wedding. The following year we headed back to California to try to make a go of it on our own.

I really had to find a good job and French/Euro cuisine was my newfound love. I was saved prior to us leaving Michigan and I was bubbling over with the power and presence of Jesus. I prayed and asked God to help me get a job. I drove down to Laguna Beach, in Southern California, and walked into this little French restaurant built on a cliff overlooking the Pacific Ocean. Victor Hugo's Inn was built in 1938 and was owned and operated by the famous Hugo family. The cuisine was exquisite - classical French cuisine at its finest. I meet Chef Pierre, and after about an hour, he hired me, right there, on the spot.

Chef Pierre taught me many things. His emphasis was on my saucier ability. He expanded my knowledge of the mother sauces and introduced me to many classical French sauces. Escoffier was my textbook and Chef Pierre was my new teacher. One of the exciting lessons I learned while working with Pierre was how to make a really great consommé. I had been making good stocks for a while and I understood the importance of a good stock as the foundation for sauces, soups, braising liquor, and court bouillons, but I had not yet made a true double consommé.

A consommé is an incredible soup. If you have ever eaten a good cup of consommé, besides its rich delightful flavor, you will notice an incredible clarity within the soup. A good consommé will have a nice golden amber color to it and the liquid will be translucent. This clearness is the mark of a great consommé. A clear consommé enables all the garnishing ingredients to stand out like jewels entrapped in fine glass. It takes skill to create a full-flavored, crystal-clear, and truly satisfying consommé.

Consommés are traditionally named after the garnish that is served with them. A consommé may also be finished with a fortified wine such as ruby Port, Madeira, or dry Sherry, as well as Cognac or even Rum. A consommé is never seasoned with ground pepper, as the pepper will make it cloudy – instead a chef my use a few drops of Tabasco. Kosher or sea salt salt may be used in seasoning.

The key to consommé consists in the clarification process. When you make your normal stock, broth, or bouillon, the liquid becomes cloudy due to the particulates and by-products that are floating in the broth. The ability to see through the stock is hindered by the food debris. The closest correlation I can use to explain this would be a comparison of the Atlantic Ocean off the New Jersey coast in contrast to the clarity of the Gulf Coast south of Anna Maria Island in Florida. Its night and day between the two – one is muddy and murky with no sign of life – the other is a crystal clear blue exposing not only an array of tropical fish but the pink coral that hugs the bottom of the ocean.

The secret to the clarification of a stock is in the preparation method. Stock is clarified by taking a ground mixture of protein, such as ground beef, combining it with whisked egg whites, and aromatic vegetables. It is the interaction between the albumin of the egg white and the particulates floating within the stock that starts to bring out the clarity. When you mix the ground beef with the mirepoix and the egg white into a cold stock, the egg whites disperse throughout the stock. As the stock, slowly heats up the proteins in the whites and the ground beef begin to coagulate. When this happens the whites reach out, gathering, or trapping all the particulates in the stock, soon they float to the top forming a raft of scum and debris. The ground beef and vegetables are there simply to fortify and enhance the flavor of the stock. After the raft is removed, what you have left in the pot is a crystal clear consommé. Sieve out the consommé and you are done.

When I was first taught how to make consommé, I was a fairly new Christian. The process of clarifying a consommé was educational for me on two levels. Obviously, the first level was learning a culinary technique on the clarification process. The second level, on the other hand, helped me grasp a spiritual truth that has helped me throughout my life – *the concept of sanctification.*

Sanctification is the process in which the Holy Spirit cleanses and renews the Christian, or sanctifies them (Acts 20:32, Romans 15:16). Sanctification is an equipping process, making us living vessels in the new spiritual temple.

> *"Therefore if anyone cleanses himself from the latter, he will be a vessel for honor, sanctified and useful for the Master, prepared for every good work."*
>
> - 2 Timothy 2:21

Two things accomplish the process of sanctification: the blood of Christ and faith in His redeeming work in us combined with the ongoing cleansing of the Holy Spirit (Ephesians 5:26, Acts 26:18). Early in my Christian walk, I had trouble understanding the ongoing work of God in my life. What I understood was performance, and I was good at that. I preformed all my life. I knew if I did well I would be loved.

Now here's the rub: that kind of thinking is opposite to the dynamics of saving grace. I knew there was nothing I could do to get God to accept me. At the same time, I had a deep desire to change and be a better person. Somehow, it did not register the way I wanted it to. It was contrary to the system of thinking that was infused in my mind. The Scriptures tell us in Ephesians chapter two, verse eight,

> *"For by grace are ye saved through faith; and that not of yourselves: it is the gift of God."*

This is where the process of sanctification steps in. Through the renewing power of the Holy Spirit, we are changed. This is an ongoing process that takes place everyday of our lives, until the moment we leave this tent of a body and see Jesus face to face.

One day while I was reflecting on the process of making a consommé, the answer came to me in a flash. Picture your life, prior to coming to Jesus, as a pile of bones in the roasting pan of life, getting toasted in the heat of life's oven. As time goes on, you hear God calling you to Himself and offering you a free gift of salvation. You struggled with this gift, thinking maybe the cost was too high and you turned your head away from God. Well God did not stop there, he had to get your attention, so He turns up the heat until your bones really started to roast and crack under the heat of life.

Finally, you responded knowing the condition and deadness of your soul. You ask Christ into your heart. In response, Jesus fills your caldron with cool, refreshing, living water to stop the burning and ease the pain. Soon thereafter, he turns the heat down to a low-slow simmer. The Father comes along and tosses in an abundance of vegetables, herbs, and spices. These are the gifts of the Holy Spirit. All of a sudden, the water in your life begins to take on a sweet aroma. It has flavor to it – so much so, that the Father smells the aroma all the way up in heaven – it was as incense in the air that filled the thrown room.

One problem though, your old nature, the dead bones from your pre-born-again life are causing the beauty of your broth to cloud and become murky. No one can see with clarity the awesome work God is doing in your life. Hence, the Father decides to remove the bones from your stock and strains them through a big China cap, passing them through the Word of God. Jesus wants you to reflect on the depth of what was happening in your life so He decides to place you under refrigeration until you are completely cooled down and in a good state of prayer and meditation. There you are, hidden in the Father's presence, learning and growing from the milk of the Word of God.

Soon the Father says to the Son, I think its time. Let's take our dear sweet broth that has been redeemed from this world and take him to the next level. That's when the Holy Spirit takes you out of the refrigerator and sets you on the prep table of life. The process of making a consommé is about to begin.

Let's look again at those ingredients for making a consommé, only this time we will define the players and their roles in the clarification process.

The Ingredients of the Clarifying Process

- **A Full Flavored Stock** – *You* – Your role is to be sanctified and conformed into His image.

- **Egg Whites** – *The Holy Spirit* - To remove all particulates in your life and give you clarity, so that people will benefit from the golden amber flavor of your broth and are touched by the gifting in your life.

- **Ground Beef, very lean** - *The Blood of Jesus* - To reinforce the power of the blood covenant that Jesus has with you - giving you power to overcome the evil one and be a life-giving force in this world to others.

- **Carrots, Leeks, Celery stalks, Tomatoes, Onion Brule** - *The Gifts of the Father* - To reinforce and heal the natural gifting that God placed in your life, at your birth that was polluted by the sin of this world – i.e., art, science, music, and so forth

- **Sachet d'Epices** - *The Gifts of the Holy Spirit* - To equip you for service in the Kingdom of God, gifts such as teaching, preaching, healing, prophecy, and miracles and so on.

- **Kosher salt, Tabasco, Cognac** - *The Gifts of the Son* - To enhance and bring out the full flavor of His life in you, so when people look into your eye they will get a glimmer of Jesus.

In my chapter on Hollandaise, I shared with you the parallel of Jesus and the egg yolk in making an emulsification. To continue that simple analogy of our dear friend the incredible, edible, egg – I want to focus on the egg white. Here we see the simple egg separated; only this time, instead of the yolk being the focus, we have the egg white. It is here that the egg white takes on the role of the Holy Spirit at work in our lives. I find this ironic because the word consommé comes from the root meaning to consume or bring to a finish. It speaks of completeness – the process of sanctifying a stock, causing a metamorphosis to take place – transforming a cloudy broth into a beautiful consommé that is fit to be served at the wedding supper of the lamb, *the consummation of all things unto Himself.*

For that reason, I want to encourage you. When the heat gets turned up in your life or you feel that things are getting tough out there – rejoice because, more than likely, the Holy Spirit is at work changing you.

God is making a consommé and the time and skill required to do this is well thought out and orchestrated to bring out all that God has for you. He wants, when people look at your life, they see right through you. There is clarity to your life. Your life has flavor to it. It has depth, warmth, and compassion. You have been brought to the point of service. You are ready to be poured out and served to a hungry world. When people taste the broth of your life they become drawn to Jesus. You become a mirror that reflects the glory of Jesus Christ to all around you.

CHAPTER 10

Dreams & Visions

As seen through strawberry cakes

"As for these four young men, God gave them knowledge and skill in all literature and wisdom; and Daniel had understanding in all visions and dreams."

- Daniel 1:17

"And it shall come to pass afterward that I will pour out My Spirit on all flesh; your sons and your daughters shall prophesy, your old men shall dream dreams, your young men shall see visions. And also on My menservants and on My maidservants I will pour out My Spirit in those days."

- Joel 2:28-29

> *"I have also spoken by the prophets, and have multiplied visions; I have given symbols through the witness of the prophets"*
>
> \- Hosea 12:10

> *"Hear now My words: If there is a prophet among you, I, the Lord, make Myself known to him in a vision; I speak to him in a dream."*
>
> \- Numbers 12:6

It's funny when you look back at your life and piece together all the milestones that were instrumental in the development of who you are. When I look back, I feel as if I am looking back at two different timelines. One is the timeline of my youth and my life prior to coming to the Lord. The other is a timeline of the events that took place after I became a Christian. The two are so different it's striking. The later feels so much a part of me I truly understand the meaning of what the Bible calls – being born again. The former appears to be someone else's life – so different are the events and the belief systems that ruled my life I have a hard time recognizing the guy that stood in the mirror of my youth.

The first year of my Christian life was truly amazing. Everything was fresh and new. I wasn't raised a Christian so I suppose my openness to experience all that I read in the Bible was never under the prejudice of being indoctrinated by some denominational belief system. The beauty of that was the ease of accepting all that I read in the scriptures in its purest and simplest form. I knew that God had no problem speaking to me with dreams and visions – it was that language that brought me to the Lord in the first place. Therefore, I was not surprised to see the Lord help me create a menu using the language of a dream.

My wife and I were two years into our marriage, living in Southern California. We were learning so much about married life, Christian life, and how to survive as a couple. Life was fun and we were adventurous – ready to do anything and go anywhere, as the Lord willed. So when I got a phone call from my cousin Jimmy asking us to move up to Canada and open a Hotel with Him, It didn't take long for us to pack our 1978 yellow Toyota and head to Vancouver, British Columbia. It was a long and wonderful drive. We stopped at so many places along the way I can't begin to tell you about it. The California coastline is so beautiful and diverse that it draws you to God by its sheer splendor.

We arrived in Vancouver and headed to Jimmy's house. Jimmy owned a couple of pubs in Vancouver so he was familiar with food & beverage operations. He had purchased an old country inn in Whistler, British Columbia, and 75 miles from Vancouver, and 7,484 feet – straight up the mountain.

Whistler had it all... majestic mountain scenery, summer glaciers, trails upon trails for hiking or mountain biking, and a charming village full of shops and restaurants. We arrived in the fall of 1979, the year before Blackcomb Mountain opened its brand new facility. We lived in a small house right on Alta Lake. It was so close to the Blackcomb ski resort – you could ski down the mountain, through the parking lot and stop right in front of our house next to the Inn.

The Inn was run down so we spent several months renovating the property to get ready for the peak ski season. Whistler was still new for a destination resort – and a far cry from what it is today. The foundation of the Inn was slowing sinking into Alta Lake, though we didn't find out until my wife was getting read to take a bath. She filled the tub with water and noticed right away a major slope from one end of the tub to the other – we laughed so hard that night I couldn't believe what Jimmy had gotten us into – a Hotel sinking into Alta Lake. They did however reinforce the foundation so we didn't fall into the lake and float away. Not that it was possible, the lake froze over in the winter with a blanket of glimmering white snow and ice that stretched out for miles. Across the lake was the other end of the mountain range and at its base was a train track that linked the two sides of the mountain.

In the winter when you looked across the lake you could see that train chugging along like a child's toy in the distance with its smoke stack bellowing-out clouds of smoke as it made its way along the base of the mountain. In the back of the inn, about ten feet from the lakefront was a hot tub. It was the most incredible feeling sitting in that hot tub surrounded by snow and trees staring across to the other side of the lake. The dichotomy of hot and cold, steam and ice was a sensation I look forward to doing it again someday.

My task was to get the kitchen ready for opening and write a menu that would be well received by the tourists. I had started writing the menu and completed the lunch and dinner sections but still had the breakfast menu to complete. That night I prayed and asked God to help me write this breakfast menu. I wanted something on the menu that was unique and innovative. I went to sleep and that night God gave me an incredible dream.

In my dream, I saw a pair of white-gloved hands working against a black background. I knew what they were doing as they prepared a dish right in front of my eyes. I saw these hands make a large pancake and set it aside. The hands grabbed some freshly sliced strawberries and mixed it with whipped sweet cream cheese. They took the strawberry and cream cheese mixture, spooned it into the center of the pancake, and folded it over taco style, crimping the edges to seal-in the mixture. The pancake was dipped into a light vanilla egg batter and sautéed in butter till golden. The pancake was turned onto a plate and topped with a caramel-pecan butter sauce, and a dollop of cinnamon whipped cream, and there you have it, a stuffed French toast pancake style. I woke up and was totally amazed at the simple creativity of the dish. It was perfect for a signature French toast item.

I thanked God for giving me the idea and I was surprised by His desire to be involved in the simple details of my life. I placed the item on the menu and it was a hit. Since that time, I have used several variations of that dish at different restaurants. That dream also was foundational in allowing me to break out of the box and focus on creating new and distinct dishes that have been the hallmark and cornerstone of my cooking ever since.

Dreams, what can you say about dreams. When I was a kid, all I ever had were nightmares, running, running, always running, trying to get away from something that was trying to snuff me out. As a mater of fact, I never started dreaming, brilliant, parabolic, colorful dreams, until I was saved, and Jesus was the center of the first dream I had, but that's another story.

Needless to say, dreams are an incredible thing. (if you want to read more about the language of visions and dreams, see my "Seer Series: The Seer's Gift; The Seer & Healing; and The Seer and Prophecy" - available on Amazon, in paperback or Kindle).

Sometimes we dream because of stress. Our subconscious mind vents thoughts that weigh us down. Other times we dream because of indigestion or the consumption of something wild like a smoked salmon pizza. Yet, many times, we dream because God desires to speak to us. God often chooses to speak pictorially, displaying His message through the language of visions and dreams. This is something He always has done and I am sure always will, or at least until we are caught up to Him.

Be it dreams, visions, feelings, thoughts, impressions, or that still small voice, God desires to invade our minds and open the doors of communication, so that we can function with Him, by Him, and through Him, in all that we do - so that we will be one as He is one. He wants us to be totally alive in Him and be used by Him, anytime and in any place -that is His goal. Jesus is calling us to put on the mind of Christ. He desires to renew our minds and cause us to be changed - to transform our thought processes in order that we think in heavenly mode and not in a fallen earthly mode, which so often binds us.

We must seek His face and as we begin to seek His face, we need to release the symbolic images of our fallen nature to Him, and replace those images with the Word of God and the eternal truth of His kingdom. Only then can the healing process begin. We will be as Brother Lawrence... practicing the presence of Christ. We will hear the word of God as we work. His words will dance upon our minds when we sleep. They will leap upon the mountaintops as we walk through the forest and the trees - enjoying the creative work of His hands. They will move as mighty visions before us as we tread upon serpents in our missionary journeys. They will lead us beside the still waters and comfort us when we are alone. His words will be active and sharper than any two edged sword and will pierce asunder the thoughts and intents of the heart's of man.

God desires to baste us in the presence of His word. He desires to envelope us in the cloud of His Shekinah Glory so that every jot and tittle of our life revolves around fellowship with Him.

Abide in Him, stay humble, and seek His face and not just His hand. Dare to be a Daniel and strive for the deeper things in Him. Don't settle for revelation, for the sake of revelation. Seek His face in the midst of revelation and you will overflow with rivers of living water - then, and only then, will your cup be a cup of blessings to others around you – and your life will be a life of strawberry cakes and dreams.

CHAPTER 11

Poverty

A call to action

"Poverty is not to be suffered in silence by the poor. Nor can it be tolerated by those with the power the to change it. The challenge is now to mobilize action - state by state, organization by organization, individual by individual."

- James Gustave Speth, UNDP

"There is something about a shared meal that brings people together. When we hand someone who has lost everything a hot meal, it blesses us. To see them take a moment of pause...mentally, emotionally and physically...and eat a delicious meal in the midst of devastation, we feel that we've made a difference that day.

– R. Gary LeBlanc, Mercy Chefs

> "World poverty is a hundred million mothers weeping ...because they cannot feed their children."
>
> - Ronald J. Sider

As a chef, I have always felt out of touch with the real devastations of those living in hunger. I am very empathic – I just feel sheltered. The abundance of food surrounds me. Daily people arrive in my restaurant eager to pay top dollar to eat our creative morsels. Because of this sheltered state, I have tried to break out of my sanctuary and walk the streets where hunger is a reality.

The day-to-day routines that fill my life tend to squeeze out those times of service. Yet, my heart wants to do something. I have to do something. I have to do this to stay in touch with the reality that 850 million people, in developing countries alone, go hungry each year. That means the devastation of hunger is no longer half a planet away, it is around the corner – it is your neighbor and mine. I am sure many Americans feel the same as I do.

According to Bread for the World, a ministry to fight hunger both on a domestic and global level:

- In the United States, 17 million children live in households where people have to skip meals or eat less to make ends meet. That means one in ten households in the U.S. are living with hunger or are at risk of hunger.

- 50 million people live in households that experience hunger or the risk of hunger. This represents one in ten households in the United States (14.7 percent). SoSA

- Nearly 14.5% households in America experience hunger: They frequently skip meals or eat too little, sometimes going without food for a whole day.

The facts about world hunger are so staggering that I find myself at a loss of what I can do or how I can make an impact to such a large problem. I believe many people feel the same way. It's like being a grain of sand in an hourglass – only time is running out and the problem keep elevating.

I know God is giving us an opportunity to reduce human suffering dramatically. We can overcome hunger if we all work together and do our part. It does not matter how small it might seem to be – to the hungry a bowl of rice can be the difference between life and death.

We have all seen the sobering faces of little African children, starving of malnutrition, as we surfed the channels on television, and some of us have even stopped suffering and listened to the heart aching stories of how a donation of a dollar a day can not only feed a starving family but give them clothing and education.

Well the truth is... it does! In the five minutes it will take you to read this chapter, 300 kids will have died in the world's poorest countries. Some of the statistics about the state of the world are overwhelming and sobering:

- Malnutrition is undermining economic growth and reducing the productivity of people trying to work their way out of poverty in the world's poorest countries. It's estimated that 2-3% of the national income of a country can be lost to malnutrition. In 2010 alone malnutrition cost the world nearly £77 billion.

- The richest 20 per cent of the world's people eat eleven times as much meat and seven times as much fish as the poorest 20 percent.

- The United Nations Food and Agriculture Organization estimates that nearly 870 million people of the 7.1 billion people in the world, or one in eight, were suffering from chronic undernourishment in 2010-2012. Almost all the hungry people, 852 million, live in developing countries, representing 15 percent of the population of developing counties. There are 16 million people undernourished in developed countries (FAO 2012).

- Asia has the largest number of hungry people (over 500 million) but Sub-Saharan Africa has the highest prevalence (24.8 percent of population).

- If women farmers had the same access to resources as men, the number of hungry in the world could be reduced by up to 150 million.

- Poor nutrition causes nearly half (45%) of deaths in children under five - 3.1 million children each year.

- The number of undernourished people decreased nearly 30 percent in Asia and the Pacific, from 739 million to 563 million, largely due to socio-economic progress in many countries in the region. The prevalence of undernourishment in the region decreased from 23.7 percent to 13.9 percent.

- Latin America and the Caribbean also made progress, falling from 65 million hungry in 1990-1992 to 49 million in 2010-2012, while the prevalence of undernourishment dipped from 14.6 percent to 8.3 percent. But the rate of progress has slowed recently.

- The number of hungry grew in Africa over the period, from 175 million to 239 million, with nearly 20 million added in the last few years. Nearly one in four are hungry. And in sub-Saharan Africa, the modest progress achieved in recent years up to 2007 was reversed, with hunger rising 2 percent per year since then.

- Developed regions also saw the number of hungry rise, from 13 million in 2004-2006 to

16 million in 2010-2012, reversing a steady decrease in previous years from 20 million in 1990-1992 (FAO 2012).

- At the beginning of the 20th century, world population was about 1.5 billion. In 1927, it reached 2 billion; in 1960, 3 billion; and in 1974, 4 billion. Nearly one-half of all people on earth will be under 25 (when). Today, people live longer and healthier than ever.

- Since 1950, average life expectancy has risen from 46 to 66 years. However, there are still a billion people - one person in six - living in poverty.

- Although the population growth rate is slowing due to falling birth rates, the absolute annual increase is still near its historic high of 86 million a decade ago.

- More than 95 percent of growth is in developing countries, with the fastest growth in sub-Saharan Africa where the average woman has 5.5 children - and parts of South and Western Asia. Population growth has slowed or stopped in Europe, North America, and Japan.

- Among the very poor, nutritional deficiencies are handed down from generation to generation like a hereditary disease.

- About one in every five babies in developing countries starts life at less than 5 lbs largely because the mother was poorly nourished.

- Almost four out of every 10, under-five-year-olds, in poor communities have stunted growth and reduced learning capacity.

- One-fifth of the world's population survives on $1 a day.

- More than 50 million people have been forcibly displaced from their homes.

Extreme poverty exists when a person is denied the opportunity to lead a long, healthy, and productive life. Extreme poverty is about a lack of opportunities. People living in extreme poverty cannot achieve their full potential because they lack things that most of us take for granted. These include safe child delivery, vaccination, health care, a caring family, education, and the ability to find a good job. A starving family has a hard time hearing the gospel of Jesus Christ because all he can hear is the pains of malnutrition.

To be successful in winning the war against poverty we must address the roots of poverty, and not immediate needs. A person who suffers from chronic disease, such as diarrhea from unclean water, cannot reach his or her potential. Nor can a young girl who is unable to go to school because of chores, or who attends a school where the teacher shows up only twice a week, and there are no textbooks.

No one wants to be sick, poor, or uneducated. The problem lies not with the poor themselves, but with their lack of opportunities. In many poor communities, schools are overcrowded and teachers are underqualified or even illiterate. If children in these schools are not learning, their parents might pull them out of school to work instead, drastically reducing their opportunities later in life. In doing so, they are likely reproducing the cycle of poverty for at least another generation.

What Can We Do As Christians?

The church needs to understand that governmental agencies and private organizations are limited in what they can do. Politics and red tape often get in the way for these organizations to contribute at their potential. Christian organizations and missionaries can be far more effective in reaching the hungry and poor of the world. The United States has limited diplomatic relationships in countries like Ethiopia. Much of the government funds used for aid has ended up in the hands of corrupt government officials to buy weapons and such.

Home-based programs through missionary organizations can be more effective since it alleviates diplomatic red tape. We need to take our lead from the scriptures. In the book of Acts, chapter six, the first program the early church set up was a food distribution center to take care of the poor in the city. The Bible talks about the compassionate distribution of food and other resources in passages such as 1 Corinthians 16 and 2 Corinthians 9. The New Testament church gave to other Christians who were in need. Here are a few things you can do to help with this issue.

Support Gary Leblanc and Mercy Chefs ministry, *(*www.mercychefs.com*).*

Serving victims, first responders and volunteers is at the core of Mercy Chefs' calling. It's a calling to show God's love and compassion by feeding those in need. Mercy Chefs is dedicated to exemplifying Christ's compassion and mercy to any and all that need assistance and relief in times of disaster and devastation. They have highly skilled Mercy chefs in Virginia, Wisconsin, Texas, Georgia, Oklahoma, North Carolina and Arizona. We have volunteers in these and many more states and are always expanding our base of volunteer chefs, cooks, industry professionals and helpers.

Start a hunger awareness program *at your church offering educational opportunities for each age group.*

Start a hunger adoption program *at your local church supporting individual children through a recognized hunger relief ministry. Post their pictures in a hallway or in Sunday school classrooms to place a face with the support.*

Set up a "Feed a Bunch Brunch" and take it to the homeless in your community.

Start a food bank or food pantry at your local church.

Inform the welfare office in your community that your church has food available for needy families.

Get a group together at your local church, rent a hall or banquet space, and treat the needy in your community to a holiday dinner.

Get involved – anything you do can help, no matter how small it might seem. Brainstorm with members of your local church and come up with your own list on how you can meet the specific need within your community.

Stir up hearts of compassion within your church by educating the congregation of the facts about hunger.

Start a hunger relief missionary program in your church.

Network with other churches in your community and start a group effort to help the hungry.

Many of the problems of poverty and hunger are not only economic but also psychological and spiritual. These include such things as poor training or wrongful attitudes, or false religions imposing destructive religious mandates on its citizens. Preaching the gospel can change not only individuals but also a culture. Just think of the impact the Hindu worldview has on countries like India.

False religious beliefs keep the Indians from utilizing beef and chicken, an important source of protein. Other ideas such as the concept of karma keep Indians from meeting the needs of the underclass. Conversion to Christianity can change not only individual lives but also a culture that rests on a false foundation.

As Christians, we need to be praying and working to provide solutions to the awesome problem of feeding the world. Please join me and ask the Lord what you can do. In the appendices of this book, there are several resources to help you get started. Please take a stand and help stop world hunger in our lifetime.

CHAPTER 12

Servants

Unsung heroes

"The gospel is like a fresh, mild, and cool air in the extreme heat of summer, a solace and comfort in the anguish of the conscience."

- Martin Luther (1483–1546)

"Do all the good you can, to all the people you can, in all the ways you can, as often as ever you can, as long as you can."

- Charles Haddon Spurgeon (1834–1892)

The restaurant industry is a large and diverse business. On a typical day in 2014, according to the National Restaurant Association, the restaurant industry posted average sales of $1.87 billion. The restaurant industry employs 13 million (10%) people in the U.S. alone, making it the nation's largest employer outside of government. More than 47 percent of today's food dollar is spent in a restaurant.

The majority of workers, in the restaurant industry, work for minimal wage, often in conditions that many people would consider not their cup of tea, surrounded by piles of dirty dishes, puddles of water on the floor, demanding guests at your table, and the never-ending line outside the door. These workers, servers, cooks, and dishwashers, these un-sung heroes, show up every day with the sole purpose to make a living and they do it by serving. When much of the world awakes on Sunday morning to attend church and head to the local restaurant for lunch or brunch, one of these "servants of the table" greets them.

The sad thing is that the wait-staff counts their success more by the varicose veins on their legs and the ach in their back than the tips in their pockets. The cooks earn their strips by the cuts and burns received during their apprenticeship. The dishwasher, the backbone of the kitchen, earns his or her strips by the sheer number of dishes one scrapes into the garbage, and all too often, by the abuse he or she takes by the few co-workers that do not seem to care or understand the importance of his duties. All of these people are the faces you see smiling back at you on Sunday morning and during the holidays.

These "servants of the table" all too often, though not all, are plagued by many a hardship. Consider the following:

- Many are un-churched, un-saved, or if saved, find it difficult to attend any kind of meaningful fellowship due to their schedule and demands of the workplace.

- Often, guests do not see them as fellow human beings but as domestic servants who must cater to there every whim, surround them. The consumer clutches onto their one or two dollar tip as if it was gold and requires the server to jump through hoops to get their mere 10 percent, all the time not realizing that the IRS is taxing them at 15 percent of their sales, wither they earn it or not.

- Many come from broken marriages and/or are single parents trying to make ends meet.

- The "Party-on Mentality" is constantly bombarding them. Many times, condoning and encouraging the consumption and over indulgence of alcohol takes place. Alcoholism and drug addiction are all too common in this industry.

- Many are at the lower-end of the economic scale and truly struggle to make ends meet.

- The education level of many consists of a high school diploma, G.E.D., or no high school at all.

- Many are of an ethnic persuasion that gives them the double duty of trying to learn English, and the job, while often working two and/or three jobs at a time to survive.

- For many, benefits like health insurance, vacation, sick leave, and retirement do not exist.

- The single mothers, after a hard day on the floor, reach in their pockets handing over most of their tips to the daycare facility, and end up working double shifts so they can live above minimum wage.

I point all this out to you because in America alone there are some 13.5 million of these "Servants of the Table." I wish to stir up in your heart sensitivity to the service workers of our land. It is time that we, the Church of Christ, stop and pray for those that work in the food service industry. It is time that we take a moment, thank them for their efforts, and reflect to them a church that is caring and understands the meaning of servant hood. It is also time that we reach into our pockets put a decent tip on the table. Shoot, bless someone that couldn't go to church by giving him or her some of your tithe. I now God would bless you for that. I believe Jesus has a special place in His heart for those in this industry. The very first miracle recorded in the book of John was a miracle for the food service worker.

> *"On the third day there was a wedding in Cana of Galilee, and the mother of Jesus was there. Now both Jesus and His disciples were invited to the wedding. And*

when they ran out of wine, the mother of Jesus said to Him, "They have no wine."

Jesus said to her, " Woman, what does your concern have to do with Me? My hour has not yet come."

His mother said to the servants, "Whatever He says to you, do it."

Now there were set there six waterpots of stone, according to the manner of purification of the Jews, containing twenty or thirty gallons apiece. Jesus said to them, " Fill the waterpots with water." And they filled them up to the brim. And He said to them, " Draw some out now, and take it to the master of the feast." And they took it.

When the master of the feast had tasted the water that was made wine, and did not know where it came from (but the servants who had drawn the water knew), the master of the feast called the bridegroom. And he said to him, "Every man at the beginning sets out the good wine, and when the guests have well drunk, then the inferior. You have kept the good wine until now!"

This beginning of signs Jesus did in Cana of Galilee, and manifested His glory; and His disciples believed in Him.

> *After this He went down to Capernaum, He, His mother, His brothers, and His disciples; and they did not stay there many days."*

- John 2:1-11

Jesus after returning from His wilderness experience went home to Galilee. Shortly after His arrival, a Jewish nobleman invited Jesus, His mother, and his disciples to a wedding. The scene was probably very much like one of our typical weddings, held in a community banquet hall or meeting place, and being a small town, everyone knew everyone. No doubt, it offered your typical entertainment package, and if I might adlib with a contemporary glimpse, it had live music, an open bar, and plenty of food to feed the guests. You can almost picture the local band playing contemporary Jewish hits as the crowd danced in celebration to the sound of the symbols and the flute. The waitstaff was skirmishing around, pouring wine, serving food, and picking up empty glasses.

The time was approaching to cut the cake and make a toast to this newlywed couple. There was one problem. One of the waiters noticed that they were almost out of wine. This would be devastating. One of Mary's friends had started this catering company and this was her first big wedding. All she wanted to do was serve them, making this wedding a memorable experience that would last the couple a lifetime. Now, her dreams of having a successful catering company lay in the balances.

She must have told Mary about her problem because Mary had approached Jesus and told Him that they ran out of wine. Jesus spoke to her briefly and she turned to the panicked wait staff and said, "*Whatever He says to you, do it.*" I can see all of them standing in the banquet hallway, out of sight of the guests, eagerly waiting instructions. Now, in the service station they had six large stone wine carafes, or water-pots, each holding a good ten gallons of liquid. Jesus turned to the servers and said, "Fill the water-pots with water."

Without hesitation, they did as he requested. Then Jesus told them "*Draw some out now, and take it to the master of the feast.*" They did as they were instructed, giving the first glass to the governor. Well when the governor looked at the wine, he was blown away. He knew he had only ordered the cheap stuff but this wine had richness about it. He studied the wine and admired its rich ruby color. He tilted his glass and swirled it slightly to release the oxygen and as he did, the hardy aroma captured his attention – with its nice subtle nutty scent. He thought if it tasted as good as it appears it appears it will be a treat indeed. He took a small amount of wine into his mouth and held it there, letting it flow over his tongue, and all around his mouth. He was thinking about the sensations on his taste buds – it was exquisite. Then panic set in, I will never be able to afford this wine, he thought.

The waiter assured the governor it was taken care of. The governor wondered where the wine had come from – but he did not know. The wait staff knew, and they thanked the Lord for such a gracious miracle. All their hard work would have been for nothing lest Christ had interceded. Here we had servants in the midst of serving – when suddenly – they ran out of their ability to serve. Jesus stepped in right at the point of their inadequacies and bridged the gap.

This was a new day upon the history of the world. The Holy Spirit chose this miracle, above all others to be listed as the first miracle in the book of John. It was the first miracle of the new covenant. When Moses, representing the law, preformed his first miracle, it was done in front all eyes – both Egypt and Israel. It consisted of turning water into blood. Jesus, the giver of mercy, grace, and forgiveness, performs this miracle behind the scenes, to the servants alone, and turns water into wine. Jesus is the suffering servant to the highest degree. He understood what they were going through and stepped in to make their efforts far better than they could have expected.

Philip and Steven were both waiters in the early church in Jerusalem (Acts 6). They were assigned the task of waiting on tables at a restaurant that the early church had formed to feed the hungry of the church community. Unlike the profit center restaurants of today – God's menu had no price – except that they love and serve Him. That was always His pattern.

In Isaiah 55:1 we read,

> *"Ho! Everyone who thirsts,*
>
> *Come to the waters;*

And you who have no money,

Come, buy and eat.

Yes, come, buy wine and milk

Without money and without price"

So what happened to these two waiters, Steven and Philip? They both had such a heavy devotion to Jesus that waiting tables became unfulfilling. They burned with the light of the glory of God and they had to tell the world about His goodness. Stephen ended up preaching the most dynamic message to the rebellious Jewish leaders in the city. They were angered so much by his heart cutting words that they put him to death and Stephan became the first Christian martyr recorded in scripture. Philip went on to be a mighty evangelist and is the only one in the New Testament that is recorded to having been transported from one location to another location, forty miles away in a matter of seconds by the power of Holy Spirit, to preach the gospel to a man who was praying for understanding.

Please join me holding up these servants of the table. They have an inheritance waiting for them and their linage is impressive. Please pray this prayer with me so that we can partake in sending out other foodservice workers like Stephen and Philip.

If you are a food service professional, chef, cook, waiter, bus-person, or just a "foodie" who loves to cook or eat and cares about the issues advanced in this book, please support or become a member of the Christian Chefs International (www.christianchefs.org). Christian Chefs fellowship is an international network of Christian cooks and chefs fellowshipping together for the purpose of encouraging and helping members grow closer to Jesus and to each other so that they may greater glorify God in all that they do.

Pray this prayer

> *Father... we humbly come before you and thank you for your tender mercy. We thank you for sending your son Jesus as the great suffering servant who died and rose again so that we might be set free. Jesus, our Lord, and Master, we thank you. We thank you with all our hearts because you did not close your eyes to the poor and needy, but opened them wide and chose to walk in our footsteps.*
>
> *We thank you that your heart is extended to the servant workers of our land. We ask you now, dear God, to touch these servants of the table. We ask you to stretch forth your hand and cause a mighty flow of your Holy Spirit to pour out in the restaurants in this land and world. We ask you to touch all those in this industry, from the hostess at the podium to the dishwasher in the back.*
>
> *We ask that you would walk through our restaurants and pour out blessings of sal-*

vation, healing, and peace to these servants of consumption and show them yourself... the Mighty Suffering Servant who is now Master and King over all creation, and move in their hearts with a desire to serve you. Father, we pray for the patrons in our restaurants. We ask you to touch those that do not know you, to draw them to yourself.

We pray for the patrons that do know you and ask that you would pour out the burden of the Lord upon there hearts and let them see the vast mission field of all those dining in our restaurants. Draw them to the last supper. Draw them to the table of showbread. Show them the bread of life. Fill them with living water. Shower them with the fruits of the Spirit. Make a place for them at the wedding supper of the Lamb. In all these things, we pray.

Amen and Amen

CHAPTER 13

Last Word

Changing food world

"For the Lord your God is bringing you into a good land, a land of brooks of water, of fountains and springs, that flow out of valleys and hills; a land of wheat and barley, of vines and fig trees and pomegranates, a land of olive oil and honey; a land in which you will eat bread without scarcity, in which you will lack nothing; a land whose stones are iron and out of whose hills you can dig copper. When you have eaten and are full, then you shall bless the Lord your God for the good land which He has given you.
"Beware that you do not forget the Lord your God by not keeping His commandments, His judgments, and His statutes which I command you today, lest— when you have eaten and are full, and have built beautiful houses and dwell

in them; and when your herds and your flocks multiply, and your silver and your gold are multiplied, and all that you have is multiplied; when your heart is lifted up, and you forget the Lord your God who brought you out of the land of Egypt, from the house of bondage"

- Deuteronomy 8:7-14

"Knowing this first: that scoffers will come in the last days, walking according to their own lusts, and saying, "Where is the promise of His coming? For since the fathers fell asleep, all things continue as they were from the beginning of creation...

...But, beloved, be not ignorant of this one thing, that one day is with the Lord as a thousand years, and a thousand years as one day.

The Lord is not slack concerning his promise, as some men count slackness; but is longsuffering to us-ward, not willing that any should perish, but that all should come to repentance.

But, beloved, do not forget this one thing, that with the Lord one day is as a thousand years, and a thousand years as one day. The Lord is not slack concerning His promise, as some count slackness, but is longsuffering toward us, not willing that any should perish but that all should come to repentance.

But the day of the Lord will come as a thief in the night, in which the heavens will pass away with a great noise, and the elements will melt with fervent heat; both the earth and the works that are in it will be burned up. Therefore, since all these things will be dissolved, what manner of persons ought you to be in holy conduct and godliness, looking for and hastening the coming of the day of God, because of which the heavens will be dissolved, being on fire, and the elements will melt with fervent heat? Nevertheless we, according to His promise, look for new heavens and a new earth in which righteousness dwells"

- 2 Peter 3:3, 4, 8-13

In this book, I have tried to paint a picture for you of the splendor of our Lord and Savior, Jesus Christ through reflections from my kitchen. We have looked at salvation through the eyes of a Hollandaise sauce. We explored sanctification expressed in the preparation of a Consommé. We glanced at the dynamics of making bread as we reflected on the mission and purpose of the Bread of Life. We have even taken a walk through my father's garden as we examined the soil of our own hearts. All of which have one purpose in mind – to draw you closer in your relationship to the Lord.

There are so many other culinary tidbits I would love to share with you but what I really want to do is encourage you to stop and listen to the small still voice of the Holy Spirit, pointing you to the everyday wonders of Jesus Christ in the world around you. Food is a joy to talk about. The culinary arts are a wonderful field to pursue. Yet, I hope I have painted a picture of priorities and have given you a sense of urgency.

We have a world that is truly spinning out of control. During the twentieth century, we have seen the growth in knowledge increase at and incredible pace. With all the advances happening so rapidly, my heart races as I ponder the events that will face us in the twenty-first century. I believe they are going to be weirder and stranger than anything we can imagine. Even the writers of fiction could never imagine the events that face us – around the corner. What lies ahead will raise issues that will effect each and every one of us. The future scientific advances will begin to put a strain on issues that are core values, as Christians - ethics, morals, and even our theological perspectives.

As a chef, I try to keep informed of the advances in bio-engineering that seem to be popping up every time we turn around. I want to know how these new sciences impact food production and development. International Bible Commentator Chuck Missler operates a ministry, The Koinonia House (www.khouse.org), which gives detailed information on science, technology, prophetic, political, national, and world events, using his extensive contacts and private sources. Chuck Missler's ministry web site is one of the best resources for staying abreast of bioengineering, DNA science, and technology.

According to Chuck Missler,

> *"Scientists have been talking about producing better foods through genetic engineering ever since the technology first became available. By mixing and matching bits of genes from one kind of organism and pasting it into another, they hoped to make new, improved plants and animals."*

Here are a few examples of what is taking place in DNA food science.

- Over the years, they've put corn genes in rice, trout genes in catfish, chicken genes in potatoes, even fireflies into tobacco (yielding a plant that actually glowed in the dark).

- A few years ago, researchers from the U.S. Department of Agriculture tried to produce leaner pork by splicing a human gene into a pig embryo. What they got was a cross-eyed porker with crippling arthritis and a strangely wrinkled face! Many may also be aware of the new genetically altered tomato, the first genetically altered food endorsed by the FDA.

- The gene-splicers have shown no shortage of imagination. Products in the pipeline include chickens that grow faster on less feed, snap peas that stay sweeter longer, bell peppers with fewer seeds and a longer shelf life, and coffee beans that have less caffeine.

There is a darker side to all this and it is so important, now more than ever, to solidify our life with Jesus and make a stand that will settle the issues of your eternity, once and for all. Consider the following:

- Among the more grotesque results in the attempts to unlock the DNA's digital code, scientists have succeeded in growing flies with large, perfectly formed eyes on the most inappropriate parts of their bodies: on their wings, on their legs, and on the quivering tips of their antennae. Some of the flies have as many as 14 eyes apiece. "This is Frankensteinian science at its best," one scientist noted.

- Researchers are telling us that some infectious and potentially lethal bacteria such as E. coli, salmonella, and Vibrio cholerae (the bug that causes cholera) exchange messages with one another in order to be dangerous.

- Lambs are now being born on a farm in Scotland, which have had their genetic construction so altered that they will produce a drug called Alpha-1-antitrypsin (AAT) in their milk.

- GenPharm International (Mountain View, California) has produced the first progeny from a Dutch biotech bull in the hopes of producing drug-manufacturing cows with a milk yield ten times that of goats or sheep.

- In Britain, researchers at the government-backed Roslin Institute are reporting progress in breeding genetically engineered chickens, which will be capable of producing drugs and vaccines in their eggs.

- Two years ago, scientists at the Massachusetts-based biotech company, Advanced Cell Technology, announced they had fused human cells into cow eggs and let them grow as an embryo for a few days. The company claimed that its aim was to culture organs and tissue in the lab suitable for transplants.

- The French have also tried cross-species experiments. Their product did not involve human genetics, but the implanting of jellyfish genes into a rabbit embryo. The result was a white rabbit, which, under a blue light, exhibited a slight greenish glow in its eyes and fur. The rabbit's cells also glowed like a jellyfish when examined under a microscope in blue light.

- Amrad, an Australian company, is reported to have taken out a European patent in 1999 on its technology, which could lead to the creation of mixed-species embryos, or human-animal hybrids. The patent covers the creation of embryos containing cells from humans, mice, sheep, pigs, cattle, goats, and fish. The details of the patent do not specify the use to which any hybrid embryo would be put, although Amrad's chief executive insisted that human cells would not be used.

- In a span of less than 15 years, the United States alone has been stricken by a wave of new infections. Toxic shock syndrome, Legionnaires disease, AIDS, Lyme disease, and hanta virus have emerged from obscurity to become household names. Infectious disease experts fear an escalation of new and possibly more deadly epidemics in the future. Indeed, some candidates already loom on the distant horizons, isolated in tiny geographical pockets.

You can see by all the advances in the biotech industry and gene sciences the next 15 years will be very interesting and should alert us to the times and the seasons in which we live. Why, all of a sudden do we see this sudden explosion of pestilence? Where are all these genetic deformities going to take us? What is at the end of this Frankensteinian research? Much of this is happening under the guise of solving world hunger and creating food stores that do not deplete, but I fear that for every advancement we make to benefit humanity – we will unleash upon this planet inconceivable horrors.

The threats of nuclear weapons are now overshadowed by the power of chemical and biological warfare. World hunger, pestilence, war, earthquakes, famine, the rise in Middle East political unrest, and the advances globalization, all point to a stage being set for the events spoken about in the book of Revelation and the book of Daniel.

My heart and desire is that you would serve the Lord Jesus. I pray that you would come to know Him and the power of His resurrection. Remember God is not a respecter of persons – he does not care about where you work, who you are, the power you have, or the names you can drop. Jesus cares about the state of your soul and the destiny of your eternity.

Give Jesus a chance and RSVP ASAP your invention at His table. The banquet He is preparing, you don't want to miss. Remember - it does not matter what you do for a living – Jesus loves you and wants you to secure your eternity with Him.

About the Author

Fred Raynaud, CEC, CCA – is an Author, speaker, and Chef by trade. He serves as the Founder and President of CELI (The Culinary Executive Leadership Institute) and the Founder of the Dreamweaver Outreach program, a street ministry bringing God's touch to the streets.

For more information please visit our website at http://www.SeersGift.com

For more information please visit CELI at http://www.CulinaryExecutive.com

With a 30+ years background driving culinary excellence, corporate culinary strategy, and guest satisfaction, Fred Raynaud supports corporate brand initiatives by seeking innovations that create differentiation and establish operational solutions and processes that bring sustainability and growth while preventing reoccurring costs from "leeching" profits from owners and stakeholders.

He strengthens organizational infrastructure by implementing key strategic culinary and business initiatives to drive a path of future-centric growth and change management. His creative mindset and vision is a key driver in building circles of innovation with his team.

The four pillars that define Chef Raynaud's management framework are Passion, Purpose, People, and Persistence.

www.ingramcontent.com/pod-product-compliance
Lightning Source LLC
Chambersburg PA
CBHW061325040426
42444CB00011B/2787